Praise for *And Now, Still*

"Reggie Marra's poetry speaks to me deeply of hope and joy, beautifully woven into the context of grief and loss. As a holistic nurse, reading Reggie's poetry reminds me of the humanity in every person. Through his life I see my life and the lives of the many patients I have touched. Reggie has the ability to gather precious moments and offer them as a gift to the reader. I recommend slowly sipping and savoring each word that it may touch and magnify your life."

- Joanna Burgess-Stocks, BSN, RN, CWOCN, Patient Advocate

"When the soul needs to be fed or held, only music and poetry are capable. I have no idea if Reggie Marra sings or plays anything – but oh, the poetry."

- Ian Percy, author, *Going Deep: Exploring Spirituality in Life and Leadership*

"Openhearted, rich in detail, and wildly irreverent, Reggie Marra's *And Now, Still* celebrates the sacred everyday connections among the living, the dying, and the dead. This intimate moment, son holding father – *I learn how heavy/ your living dead weight can be/ face to face, chest to chest* – is one example of the brave, unflinching nature of Marra's work.

"And from the title poem these lines – *I feel etched stone's/ temporary permanence,/ time, laughter, conversation,/ ...first and final truth/ lost shinanklefoot,/ ...two key turns, a silent sister* – reminding us that all emerges from and gives way to silence, the mysterious center point, this moment. And so the poet mourns and sings. Lyric to narrative, journal entry to rant, his layered language, its poetic intelligence, invites deeper presence. A generous collection that defies being boxed, this book is a healing journey offered by a kind, resilient, skillful and eloquent guide."

- Janet E. Aalfs, author of *Bird of a Thousand Eyes*, founder & director of *Lotus Peace Arts*

Praise for *This Open Eye: Seeing What We Do*

"*This Open Eye* is a powerful, devastating, and stunningly beautiful book. Reggie Marra has unfalteringly absorbed the images and voices of the war in Iraq, pared them down to the bone, and handed them back to us that we, too, might bear witness to our times. Not in any of these poems, or the essay, has he taken the easy way out. Like Breyten Breytenbach, Nelly Sachs, and Antonio Machado before him, Marra reclaims the essentially human from both the brutal and the brutalized."
- Trebbe Johnson, author of *The World is a Waiting Lover: Desire and the Quest for the Beloved;* founder, http://www.radicaljoyforhardtimes.org/

"Reggie Marra writes with stunning, graphic precision – brutal scenes the American news skips over, scenes of endless sorrow that politicians bury under false phrases like 'total victory.' I read these small but huge poems with a chill of recognition and gratitude – thank goodness for poets like Reggie Marra who look deeply and care even more deeply about telling the truth. These poems are tributes to the nearly-invisible wounded and the honest humanity so many of us yearn for now."
- Naomi Shihab Nye, author of *Transfer* and *You & Yours;* National Book Award finalist for *19 Varieties of Gazelle*

"Reggie Marra captures the tragedy of war from all angles. His vision expands beyond gender and race to embrace our common humanity. Unafraid to depict the graphic consequences of hate, uninhibited in his words by the politics of aggression, Reggie bravely steps into the epicenter of world conflict and individual suffering. He captures the colors of youth and the mud of death, creating a dichotomous reality that has brought poets and artists to their knees since the dawn of civilization. Reggie is the journalist of our times. His poetic images will be remembered for centuries to come."
- Eileen Albrizio, author of *Messy on the Inside; Rain, Dark as Water in Winter* and *On the Edge*

(Really) Early Praise & Motivation

"Excellent! This has an extraordinary quality that not half a dozen of your class achieved. Your language is simple, but your sentence + idea structure is quite complex."
- Br. Jerome Stevens, FSC, PhD, December 1, 1970

During my junior year at Sacred Heart High School, our principal, Br. Jerome, "guest lectured" in my English class on Thursdays. He was the only member of the faculty/administration who had a doctorate, so for me, it was a big deal. During one of his visits he asked us to compare two things that appeared to be different. I chose Christmas and death (hey, I was sixteen). The original poem, entitled "Christmas, a Time of Sorrow" with his handwritten comment, appears on the final page of this book.

After the publication of the first edition of The Quality of Effort *in 1991, while I was processing mail orders by hand, I noticed his signature on a check from De La Salle Collegiate in Michigan, where he was principal. We began an intermittent correspondence that faded after 2006, but that allowed me to express my gratitude for his encouragement and to send him copies of my first two volumes of poetry.*

I know now that he saw something that I did not, and perhaps could not, see in myself at sixteen. In this same year, I met Jerry Houston and heard Kristofferson for the first time. Each of these encounters continues to play an essential role in my life.

Also by Reggie Marra

Poetry

Who Lives Better Than We Do? (2001)

This Open Eye: Seeing What We Do (2006)

Prose

The Quality of Effort: Integrity in Sport and Life for Student-Athletes, Parents and Coaches (1991)

Living Poems, Writing Lives: Spirit, Self and the Art of Poetry (2004)

The Quality of Effort 2nd Edition (2013)

The Quality of Effort Workbook (2013)

Living Poems, Writing Lives: A Path to Healing and Wholeness
Forthcoming (2018)

And Now, Still

Grave & Goofy Poems

And a Bit of Prose

REGGIE MARRA

From the Heart Press

2016

Copyright © 1997, 2001, 2007, 2012, 2014, 2015, 2016 by Reggie Marra

All rights reserved.
Published in the United States of America by From the Heart Press, an imprint of Integral Journeys.

And Now, Still
ISBN: 978-0962782879
Library of Congress Control Number: 2015908187

Earlier editions of select poems in the "He Could Spin a Yarn" and "She Rarely Let Him Finish" sections of this book appeared in *Who Lives Better Than We Do?* (2001) and appear here with permission of the author. "When I Make Myself Small," and "The Old Lesson Again (and Again)" originally appeared in Vol. 3, Issue 3 of *The Wayfarer: A Journal of Contemplative Literature*, and appear here with permission of the author.

"Your Face" words and music by Cliff Eberhardt. Copyright © 1984 Cliff Eberhardt Music / Aixoise Music, ASCAP. All rights reserved/Used by permission.

Cover design and photograph by Reggie Marra.
Author photo by Reggie Marra, Lu Mix and Tri Pod.

More information:
http://reggiemarra.com/
http://qualityofeffort.com/
http://livingpoemswritinglives.com/
http://www.teleosis.org/

For Noé Jiménez,
artist and good man, aka *Jim Enez*,
who drew a three-dimensional *Star Wars* All-Terrain
Armored Transport (AT-AT) to scale when he was 8.
He lived through some of these poems,
and lives an intentional life. Thanks, ~~Jim~~ Noé.

And for Jay Stearns, John Cusano,
Paul Tepikian and Michael Sallustio,
aka *Stearns, Gianni Boy, Mr. Tepikian,* and *Migelooch*,
for reasons each of them understands.

CONTENTS

Holiday Death Math   1

He Could Spin a Yarn

Worth a Shit   5
Day of Hearts   7
A Goddamn Leg   11
Nursing Home Goodbyes   12
The Hall Closet in Winter   13
The Other Side   14
Selected Journal Entries   15

She Rarely Let Him Finish

New Tricks   41
Sanitize Your Pores   43
Dialysis Days   45
November 16, 1999   47
November 19, 1999   49
November 22, 1999   51
What Else?   53
December 2, 1999   55
We All Want Her   57
What Do You Want to Do?   58
4:32 PM   60
The Ingredients   63
Christmas Spirit   65
The Dance We Always Share   67
"Tidied"   69
Resurrection   71

She Created Beauty

Bump	77
(Some of) Her Own Words	80
Creation Continues	81
Remembering Is Preferable	83
Please Don't Abandon Me	84
Still on the Bed	85
The Sniper	88
Awaiting the Judges	90
13 Ways of Looking at Wells Fargo	92
Five Years Later	108

And Now, Still

And Now, Still	113
Nuclear Family	117
Writing Again	119
Surprised by Grief	122
Nursing Home Return	124
The Rickety Bridge	125
The Wound	127
When I Make Myself Small	129

First Family

Fillet of Soul With a Dark Night Glaze	133
Freedom	140
You Stood Up	142
Knowing	144
The Old Lesson Again (and Again)	146
Afterwordledgements	149
About the Author	151

Everyone forgets that Icarus also flew.

   - Jack Gilbert, "Failing and Flying"

If you don't break your ropes while you're alive,
do you think
ghosts will do it after?

The idea that the soul will join with the ecstatic
just because the body is rotten –
that is all fantasy.
What is found now is found then.
If you find nothing now,
   you will simply end up with an apartment in the City
     of Death.
If you make love with the divine now, in the next life
     you will have the face of satisfied desire.

   - Kabir, translated by Robert Bly

Ain't afraid of moonlight
Ain't afraid of freedom
Blood'll make you crazy
But your soul'll keep you sane

Sailing to the starlight
Over the horizon
Open to the pleasure
Equal to the pain

   - Kris Kristofferson, "Closer to the Bone"

HOLIDAY DEATH MATH

My father left a leg-and-a-half along
with the rest of his 88-year-old body
on Valentine's Day, 1996. My mother
dropped her 83-year-old multiple-
bypassed heart, dialysized kidney and
early colon cancer between the turkey
and the tree on December 15, 1999,

30 days before my January 15, 2000
wedding and 10 years and 9 months
before my sister slowed, then
brought her heart to zero on St. Patrick's
Day, 2009, three-quarters through her 55th
year, leaving 9,000 Cardizem nanograms
in her still tired blood. And me, my hips

are only 12 years old in my 61st year and
I've got long-term plans for them and some
200-plus bones and assorted organs, but I
can't help notice that February 14, December
15, and March 17 scream for January 16 and
they're screaming directly at me, albeit
without a specific year. And while the day
after my anniversary means less now that
I'm no longer married, with not quite 13
years of marriage and the continuing education
of divorce, I feel I'm beginning to understand
some things, and in no hurry to go anywhere
without this body, especially to fulfill a

coincidental family death sequence or
arbitrary arithmetic progression. Of course,
their 75-year average age of death is just six

tenths of a year lower than statistical U.S. males, and I could bump that to 80 with a sex change or deeper embrace of my feminine side, or to 79 by

becoming Japanese. These trajectories land somewhere between 2029 and 2034, but my father smoked for 70 years and made it to 88, albeit minus half-a-leg but with original hips, and I've never smoked, have a resting pulse of 58, total cholesterol 169, triglycerides 56, and I've been laughing more than 50 years – long before Norman Cousins prescribed it. Shit. I might live forever. The Grim Reaper will be a Grin Reaper when I'm done with her. I eat fillet of soul with a dark night glaze *and* midnight chocolate cake, I know I'm vast emptiness, eternal presence and original face, and that

infamous Buddhist hot dog vendor can't make me one with everything because I always, already am.
And with relish.
To boot.

He Could Spin a Yarn

WORTH A SHIT

We take turns kissing
her goodbye at the
bedside. I'm first,
then dad, and we
walk down the hall
toward the elevators.
He steps in as the
doors slide open,
I follow, they
close, he says
If we lose her,
I'm not gonna' be
worth a shit.
My mind races.
I put my arm around his shoulder.

Neither *You're right, you*
won't be worth a shit, nor
Sure you will – you'll still
be worth a shit, at
the very least, seems an
appropriate response.

Our descent ends,
doors slide open, and
I remember more of
who he is – the man
the Sea Bees
and Marines called
Joker on the Gilbert and
Mariana Islands, who
somehow worked a
New York pipe wrench

through his seventy-
first year.

She'll be fine,
I say, *and you'll always
be worth at least
a shit to me.*

He almost suppresses the smile.
Says nothing. We walk to
the car. She survives him
by almost four years.

DAY OF HEARTS

At eighty-six the room spun,
the hand numb, the heart hurt,
no real hope, the doctor
says   completely
unprepared, we prepare
for your departure.

A plum to a prune
you shrink in bed,
feet and toes blackening,
we choose to lose the leg
and keep you, you,
oblivious to it all.
Hope we're right
or at least good.

Suddenly awake,
birds and trees only you can see,
stump that everyone sees but you
in plain sight,
minor stroke, a gift perhaps
to tame the trauma
somewhat.

Eighty-six with a big piece missing
still feel the shinanklefoot,
seeing, not believing –
not seeing, feeling
what's gone.

You grope instinctively,
an imaginary breast pocket in
the flimsy, bare-assed gown

for the trusty pack of butts.
Asleep, bring two fingers to your mouth,
take a long, slow drag on an imaginary weed
again and again and again

until deep breath
itself satisfies the craving.
Awake, you want a drag,
want a puff, want a butt.
You realize something is amiss –
want to walk: No.

We tell you the story,
months pass,
you understand slowly,
one word at a time:
Who would've wished this on me?

Frustrated,
need to piss,
need to shit,
just go in the diaper, they say
fuck that, you say
good answer, I say.
Who would've wished this on me?

I learn how heavy
your living dead weight can be
face to face, chest to chest
my arms under yours around my neck,
three feet on the floor hovering above the bowl,
seeing, feeling, hearing, tasting, smelling,
breathing
each other, reversing roles
through layers of folds and wrinkles

I learn to wipe you clean,
you apologize for false alarms,
we laugh when you say
it's *a real pain in the ass.*

The nursing home,
a euphemistic *we can't get it done,*
you fall three times from the
bed and wheelchair in the
first one thousand, four hundred forty minutes,
a swollen-eyed and bloody-nosed TKO –
fight far from over though,
head nurse quoting restraint-free environment,
me, threatening,
you, finally restrained.

You learn the wheelchair life,
tell stories, remember laughter,
demand *a goddamn leg*
and get it –
arthritic, swollen,
bone-on-bone hands and shoulders,
shrunken, bowed and shriveled
leg-and-a-half,
limiting the minutes you can lean
on the walker, but
lean and limp you do.

One hundred and four weeks.

Awake at eighty-eight: pneumonia.
A shadow dissolving at dusk,
bedridden again, wordless,
nod to my questions,
acknowledge my hand on yours.

A phone call next morning in class,
I know.
The ninety-second walk, the
gleaming tile floor, the office,
I wonder how to be,
joke with the hoop coach,
pick up the phone and
Becky tells me gently.

On this 1996
roses and chocolates and
I love you Day of Hearts:
yours stops.

A GODDAMN LEG

Kathy gently supports you
touching triceps through
the turquoise sleeve as
you step determinedly and
gingerly forward, hands
tight on the walker, nursing
home ID's strapped to each
wrist and that ludicrous
velcro-fastened ersatz sandal
on your infected right foot,
allowing gauze-wrapped
toes to breathe.

The real action unfolds
where the rolled up left
pant leg exposes the sock-
padded stump resting in
and fastened to the prosthesis'
white cup ending in the metal
tube and fake foot that fits
into the gray and white
Velcro-strapped
running shoe.

NURSING HOME GOODBYES

Against the front lobby's silver-
white-and-no-haired backdrop,
so many wheels in motion
sitting down, our goodbye kiss
already gone, I wave and watch
you wave goodbye again and again.

Each twilight lobby window wave
suggests we can't get it done
until your still   perfect   breathless
body alleviates our well-intentioned
ignorance.

THE HALL CLOSET IN WINTER

Brown corduroy Levi's jacket
with fake fleece lining,
my gift of youth
on your seventy-fifth birthday.
Unsure if you like it,
I monitor the time it spends
in the hall closet in winter and
the time it spends on your back.
My great joy is your embrace of
warmth, youth and love
with a Levi's tag.

Thirteen winters later,
the jacket hangs in
the thin closet, room W 119A,
your two-year home without the leg.

Now, eight months after we lose you
I stand with high school kids
outside three vans, amid
steaming soup and coffee
sandwiches and used clothes,
the men who live in Central Park,
and I don't see who gets the brown
corduroy with the fake fleece and the
Levi's tag. Not sure I want to –
better, perhaps, knowing its embrace
without knowing whom.

I'll see him next run, maybe
tell him it was yours –
see if he understands
my joy it's not hanging in
the hall closet in winter.

THE OTHER SIDE

Their home regresses
to a house when he dies,
leaves her twice as much
room, endless silence,
saddest space and sound
she'll never fill or hear

The yard sprouts grass
   that needs cutting   leaves
     need raking   shrubs
       need pruning

The car grows an engine
        that needs oil, plugs and coolant
   brakes   once simply stopped
now plead for pads and fluid

Snow demands shoveling
  gutters   cleaning
   garden   planting
    garbage a trip to the curb

The living room recliner near the bookcase
  kitchen chair near the back door
    bedside closest to the window
     develop vacancy
      remember occupancy. But

his disappearance soothes her failing vision
his silence calms her hearing loss
his stilled heart unburdens hers so quiet now
his spirit   free   at last   flows fully into hers
      still captured in this life.

Selected Journal Entries

October 11, 1992

    The hand. How could the hand do this to him after all these years? The hand that guided the toothbrush, and later inserted and removed the dentures, moved the pen across the paper when he signed his name, shifted the gears in the truck, swung the hammer, pushed and pulled the saw, turned the screwdriver and helped torque the wrench, placed him under oath, made the sign of the cross, guided the sixteen-pound ball toward a 174 average, swung half the golf club, pushed half the lawnmower, usually had the upper hand while raking leaves and shoveling snow, took turns holding the hands of those he loved, occasionally whacked the younger ones on the rear end, rubbed his eyes, scratched his head, shared half the load when he pulled on his socks and pants, tied his shoes, carried the trash cans to the curb, dug the garden, planted seeds, tied the plants to the stakes, and proudly, lovingly picked the vegetables when they were ripe.

    The hand had gently supported the kids' heads and necks when they were infants, it had changed their dirty diapers and rocked them softly to sleep; the hand had shaken thousands of other hands – many familiar, and many new and never to be shaken again; it had waved goodbye and hello; wiped away tears – his own and others'; saluted Naval officers in the Pacific during World War II and waved in disgust toward the television at political leadership's oxymorons.

    The arthritic hand gradually found simple tasks increasingly painful, but the heart never allowed mere physical pain to prevent a task's completion. So the hand did things more slowly, less comfortably, and only abandoned what was not essential. It rolled the final ball in the final frame down the alley at Scappy's, teed up the final ball on the 18th tee at Sprain Lake, but remained intimate with the hammer and the wrench, the broom, the rake and the hose, and of course, tea, cookies, and Biddie.

Then one day during the hand's 85th year, while trying to manipulate the fork at Anne Marie and Joseph's anniversary dinner at Traveler's Rest, the hand refused to work. At first he tried to use it anyway, without the feeling, but the best that he could do was to push the food around on the plate. He tried to grasp the handle on the dainty coffee cup, and was wise enough to enlist the left hand's help. Awkward and arthritic as well, despite years of playing second fiddle, the left hand pitched in with its best effort.

Anything but ask for help. Anything but complain. Especially at the anniversary dinner. Nothing to worry anyone about. But we were watching. I asked if I could help with anything; he assured me everything was fine. When he got up to use the men's room and didn't return after ten minutes, I went looking for him, expecting to find him outside having a smoke, but not entirely free of the fear of finding him passed out on the men's room floor. I checked the stalls. Nothing. I walked outside into the chilly October evening air. "Everything all right?" "Yeah, just wanted to have a smoke."

Two days later the numbness got bad enough to convince him to ask for help. St. John's. Left-side carotid artery blockage, angioplasty, dangerous at his age, close to the brain. A week of disorientation and confusion. Not sure if he'd suffered a minor stroke or if some dye had found its way to the brain. He couldn't concentrate, couldn't remember, lost focus in the middle of sentences, tried to find the words, couldn't, got frustrated, then angry. And then it gradually came back.

Slowly, surely, he could find it again. They went ahead with the carotid bypass and he came home, tired, weak, but home nonetheless, with a cleaned out carotid artery – the surgeon unclogs the plumber's pipes.

Thursday: December 30, 1993

The 6:50 call gave me the opportunity to see a stunning early morning moon through gaps in the large, snow-covered evergreen outside my bedroom window on Pryer Terrace. Sun not yet up, sky brightening, post lamps still lit – beautiful morning, clear sky with just a few scattered clouds left from the storm.

For good or ill, the soundtrack from *Les Miserables* accompanied me as I warmed up the car in the parking garage across from Rice Hall. On the way to Yonkers and St. John's, I heard "Drink With Me" first – asking, "Could it be your death means nothing at all..." followed by Cosette telling Valjean that no, Papa, it's not your time yet.

Almost two weeks earlier, on December 19, while driving east across the Tappan Zee Bridge, I had taken a long look toward Yonkers and the water tower atop Executive Boulevard to my right – south and a little east. I could see the hospital, and thought of the great views of the river and the Palisades that it provided, views I'd seen far too often, and I realized that I'd never seen the early morning, but only the later day sun on the cliffs from the hospital's windows. This morning I saw the early morning sun on the snow-covered cliffs. The river dark and flowing, the sky clear, and the jagged stone bathed in a warm, bright glow. I saw all this because they called and said he's dying.

I'm sitting with mom now at 12:15 PM in the surgery waiting room outside the critical care unit. Yet another great view of the Hudson, the Palisades and the bridge to the north. Dr. Schwartz was here earlier – at the same time as Anne Marie,

Joseph, Uncle Frank, Aunt Nora and Uncle Jimmy. He spoke of dad's "tired heart" and was honest enough to say that he didn't have a lot of hope. He's been good and honest for a long time; it must be difficult to bring such news after years of providing care for patients.

Saturday: January 1, 1994

It's been a challenging forty-eight hours. The emotions involved in watching my father die gradually are strong, positive, sad and much else that I have yet to identify. I came here, *we* came here, at the urging of the professionals, expecting it to be his last morning. Thursday wasn't; Friday wasn't; the jury is still out today.

He had no responsiveness other than reflex these past two days – hands gripping, eyes open but unfocused, twitches, expressions of what looked like pain. This morning's call convinced me again that this was it, and when I arrived, no one else was in the room. I took his hand and said, "Hey, Dad," and he opened his eyes, looked at me and smiled. He nodded yes and no to questions. When Mom and Anne Marie walked in I said, "Talk to him – he'll respond," and they just looked at me. Then they did; and he did.

He's been in and out since then. Around 3:00 PM I had his hand in mine and he opened his eyes and mouthed "I love you." I said "I love you too." He mouthed "Thanks." I said "You're welcome." He smiled. Polite family we are.

I wonder if his dawning awareness is a response to his deteriorating condition. Kidneys are weak, circulation is bad – little or no pulse below the knees. I can't help feeling that he's fighting like a bastard because he *knows* that fighting is the goal now; I wish he knew that letting go is okay too (as if *I* know that, or know that he doesn't). It is difficult in the moment at times to live the truths we embrace in the "big picture." I have this jumble of emotions now – for him, Mom, Anne Marie and Joseph – for all of us. I feel on the brink of a great loss and a great gift simultaneously.

January 1994 (no date specified):

The Memory

What had happened? The question hovered – consumed every thought, action, breath – then hovered some more. Sure, they had told him over and over and over again. December 26 lightheadedness, Frank's taking him to the hospital, Biddie's having a bad cold so she couldn't come to visit, her phone calls from home: "I love you." "I lowve you." "I love you." "I love you too, three, four, five…"

Then nothing – or next to nothing. Vague memories of people coming and going, one-way conversations, great discomfort, and tubes and hoses and straps and hunger and thirst and confusion – a relentless desire to tell them something, anything, but only able to sort of wink a little – kind of nod a bit – not sure if they saw or understood.

Something was wrong – different. He knew it as soon as he woke up, but he had no idea what it was. Just a feeling. He didn't understand the straps on his wrists that connected him to the side rails of the bed, the straps that kept him from scratching his nose or rubbing his eyes, or with the grace of God, taking a long, slow drag on a butt. "Tethered" they called it. Occasionally one of them would say "restrained," but that always earned severe looks and momentary silence from the others. And his throat was still so dry.

Finally, gradually, they let him drink from a straw and eat some pureed foods, and pissing was no problem because the catheter had been there forever, and shitting was no problem, at least at first, because they said to just go in the diaper and someone would clean him up. Yeah, but they didn"t have to lie in it for five minutes, or forty, or an hour. He wondered about the garden and the battery in the car and the remote for the garage door because they all needed to be taken care of. But then he forgot. Again.

Wednesday: January 12, 1994

The Leg

The leg. How could they do this to the leg after all these years? The leg, without whose perfectly timed depression and release of the clutch pedal the hand would never have been able to shift so smoothly. The leg that kept its foot firmly on the ground – the stabilizing force for the genuflection's reverence, the bowling ball's release and the golf swing's follow-through. The leg that favored every other ladder rung.

On Monday at around 1:00 PM the doctors amputated his left leg about four inches below the knee. I wondered if it would be more accurate to say he gave them the leg so he could live, but that's not what happened. He's rarely been communicative since December 29. A few moments, literally seconds, of alleged recognition and a nod or a smile (or what we think is a smile – it's hard to tell with all the tubes and tape and his teeth out) is what we've had to work with. To the best of our knowledge, he doesn't know the leg is gone, and if and when he wakes up he's going to find out – maybe all alone, maybe with company – but he'll find out. Whose idea was *this?* That's what I'd want to know.

He's been on morphine since they took the leg. That was my point above – he didn't give it; they took it – you can't have given something you don't even know is gone. Two weeks of unresponsiveness – respirator, pacemaker, morphine, nitroglycerine, catheter, stomach pump, "Trauma-Cal" and what have you – they give you all of that and take your leg for the same reason. What? To keep you alive? To make you comfortable? To reduce your pain?

There is Hope and there are hopes. The hopes seem to hinge upon what would make *us* happy. What about *him?* If courage is grace under pressure, grace implies a certain dignity. I'm not convinced of the dignity of his current situation. The purpose of all in ICU can be legitimate – to sustain life. It's the meaning that gets confusing. What exactly is *life?* (*there's* an original question). Who is any one of us to determine that? This is the paradox: there is a selfishness both in wanting him to "live" and in hoping he will die with peace and dignity, rather than live in pain, frustration and feelings of uselessness and burden – but that's *my* bias. What about him? Which is the real courage? Wrong question. Which courage would he choose? The courage to battle and fight and not quit despite the pain and frustration, or the courage to accept what he can't change – I guess serenity itself is a type of courage. Which is the love he would choose – to fight and deal with the pain and frustration in order to have more "time" with his loved ones; or to accept the time he has and to spare his loved ones the pain and burden of his frustration, pain and impending death?

What about him? Does he have any idea what's going on? Does he think he's dying? Is he afraid? Sorry? Joyful? Ready? Impatient? Pissed off? Confused? Frustrated? Oblivious?

We can plan to widen doorways and build ramps; the doctors say he'll be here at least another six weeks. He hasn't been consciously communicative in two. How did they decide on six? Magic? An honest "We just don't know" may have been better. The reality of his resilience – toughness – in the past can be a real challenge too. How many more times can he bounce back? Once? Twice? No more? When *is it?*

Sunday, January 16, 1994

They took him off the respirator this morning. He looked more relaxed, but his wrists are still tethered, he's getting oxygen, and his responsiveness to our presence is still limited. He doesn't know about the leg yet. The doctor told him he's been in the hospital through some serious conditions and surgery and that he's getting better. I don't know. Much of the machinery is gone, but he's so shriveled up and wrinkled from lying there – I guess a combination of atrophy and weight loss. If his body strengthens, we're going to see a real question of will. "And what is good, Phaedrus, and what is not good—need we ask anyone to tell us these things?"

They're talking now of the possibility of chopping off part of his right leg too; the circulation is bad and the toes are still black, although some signs of improvement are evident. Mom and I spoke this afternoon outside the social services office. She said she wanted to give them permission to take the right leg if they think it's necessary.

"Why would we do that?" I ask.
"What do you mean?"
"What are we trying to accomplish by taking another leg?"
"We're trying to save Daddy's life."
"So he can wake up at 86 with no legs and have no idea what happened?"

Her eyes fill; mine are a drop behind. "But what else can we do?" she asks.

"Think about him for a minute. Right now we're thinking

about us – we'll be able to sleep better if we do everything we can to keep him alive – but what's alive? Would you want to wake up at 86 and find your legs gone?"

"So you think we should let him die?"

"No. I think we should think. I don't know what the right thing is; I don't know if there is a right thing to do. But I wonder where we'll stop – two legs; two legs and an arm; both legs and both arms? So he can wake up a head and a torso? He signed a living will years ago – no extraordinary means – if the hospital had the DNR on file he might have gone already. I have to think that amputating the leg of an 86-year-old man without his knowledge is an extraordinary step."

We hug. Sit together in silence.

Sunday, January 23, 1994

He spoke to me (or someone invisible in the room) yesterday and today. He's had a minor stroke and has fleeting short-term memory. He says some things I can't decipher and when I ask him to repeat them or I say, "What?" he looks at me as if I'm stupid (not just me – anyone who doesn't understand). He makes this surprised, exasperated, impatient face – and then can't remember what he was trying to say.

Yesterday one of the nurses said, "Reg, see you later."

He says, "alligator."

....

Today he keeps staring at the ceiling and pointing, and says something like, "that's ridiculous," and I search the room for what's up there, can't find anything, and ask him *what* is ridiculous. He gives me the look, followed by "the *birds*," as he points again. They must be small and quick because I never see them.

....

Later on he looks at me and says, "Tree."

I'm gullible, so I say, "What about a tree?"

His response: "I think that I shall never see a poem lovely as a tree," plus the next two lines of Joyce Kilmer's poem, which he probably learned in high school some seventy years ago.

Wednesday, March 2, 1994

On February 24 at approximately 12:30 PM they discharged Dad from the hospital and shipped him to Shalom Nursing Home in Mount Vernon. February 24, 25 and 26 were nightmares of sorts. Just reacting to the nursing home itself – the sights, sounds, odors and general feeling of the unknown. Then he fell twice from the wheelchair on Friday and once from the bed on Saturday. I found him on the floor, bloody nose and cut around the eye, and then debated "restraint-free environment" with a steady stream of staff. They restrained him.

He's more coherent now than he's been in the last few weeks. Strange feelings. More on this – more detail – as I figure it out, think about it.

Monday, March 14, 1994

Today we moved Dad from Shalom to Cabrini Nursing Home in Dobbs Ferry. He was born, and lived his first forty-five years, less the time in the Pacific during World War II, in Dobbs Ferry. More coincidentally, in his late sixties, he was on the team of plumbers that built Cabrini. Brighter and more spacious than Shalom, Cabrini offers beautiful views of the Hudson and the Palisades, and is a shorter, simpler commute for most of the family and friends who might visit. For Dad, it seems to be just another place away from home, albeit one he remembers.

❦ ❦ ❦

Easter Sunday, April 3, 1994

I asked Dad today what we could do for him. His reply: "Just be happy."

Tuesday, May 17, 1994

Resilience

Even though we've told him in detail about the leg – the whole story, we're still not sure if he understands or remembers, or how much he understands or remembers. He and I are sitting on the patio in front of Cabrini, facing Broadway, the sun feels good, we're watching the cars and people go by, he's sitting there looking so fragile and tiny and helpless, and neither of us forces a conversation, just enjoying the warmth, being outdoors, being together – being.

"I don't know who would've wished this on me," he says.
"What do you mean?"
He gestures toward where his left foot used to be. "My foot. Who would've wished this on me?"
"I don't think anyone would wish it on anyone," I say. "Do you remember what happened?"
"It fell off."
"Where did it fall off?"
"I think it was in front of the house," he says.
"Was it an accident, you mean?"
He gets a little frustrated. "*I* don't know. I don't think it was an accident."
"Would you like me to tell you the story again? Do you want to know?"
"*Yeah,* I want to know."
"On December 26 you felt lightheaded, so Uncle Frank came and took you to the emergency room at St. John's. Both you

and Mom had bad colds so she couldn't go out. They admitted you, just as a precaution, and said they wanted to run some tests. You felt better once you were there, but they admitted you anyway.

"On the 29th you had a severe angina attack – everything shut down, so they put you in ICU and hooked you up to a respirator and a pacemaker and God knows what else, and you developed blood clots in your feet and then gangrene, and they told us that if they didn't amputate your left leg below the knee, the gangrene would spread and kill you. It should have been your decision to make, but you were unconscious for two weeks so we had to make it for you. We wanted you to live, but we didn't know if you would want to wake up at 86 and find that your left leg was gone, so we debated back and forth and finally said to take the leg, and we hoped it was the right thing or at least a good thing to do.

"So they took the leg and your heart got stronger and you gradually improved, and one by one they took away the tubes and hoses and even the straps until you were doing it on your own again, just like you had for 86 years."

We sat momentarily in silence, and then I asked, "What do you think you would have chosen if you were conscious?"

He sat and thought for the better part of a minute, picking at the pills on his favorite old brown polyester pants (that Mom hated), then looked at me and said with great clarity, "That's a really hard choice to have to make. I don't know what I would've done." Perfect response.

We sat in silence again for a while.

☙ ☙ ☙

Wednesday, November 16, 1994 (87th Birthday)

A Short Walk to the Kitchen

What's really on my mind, in my heart, and probably in the deepest part of my soul is not our respective memories of events, but what the experience is like for him. What was it really like when he *visited* his home of forty years after eight-and-a-half months away? How did it feel from the wheelchair to see that shady corner in front of the tool shed, where he would sit and rest beneath the old maple he'd planted decades ago, sipping an iced tea and enjoying a butt, in a break from mowing, raking, digging, watering, tying the plants or painting the deck?

Does he miss the simple pleasure of enjoying some golf, or the Yankees or whatever Mom wanted to watch, from the comfort of the recliner where a cup of tea and a Stella D'Oro Breakfast Treat or some anisette toast or some chocolate chip or oatmeal cookies or a small dish of vanilla ice cream was a short walk to the kitchen away? Where he could get up and walk to the picture window and look out to see whose car was making all the noise or parked facing the wrong way, which nobody cared about anymore, not even the cops?

And what about the prosthesis? The doctors were against it, thinking it would be a waste for him, but he insisted and persisted, and we backed him up, so they fitted him this week, and he says to Uncle Frank, "I want to get this thing on so I can help Biddie shovel the snow this winter." He's certain he'll be able to walk again; the doctors doubt it, but having experienced both his resilience and the doctors' cautious pessimism in the past, I wonder how this will play out. The walker will be tough on his hands and shoulders with all the arthritis, but he was 'supposed' to be dead on January 1, and now it's November and he got a bronze medal in the free-throw-shooting contest at the

County Center, got dressed up as Tootsie for Halloween (Mom's idea, not his), and is talking about shoveling snow once he gets his "goddamn leg" as he likes to call it.

Friday, August 18, 1995

    We're sitting in the third-floor solarium listening to Sal and his friend sing and play the mandolin and guitar, and Dad leans over, taps me on the arm and asks, "What's the name of that river out there?"

    I immediately know I won't win wherever this goes, but I answer anyway. "The Hudson."

    He raises his eyebrows. "You, too?"

    "What do you mean?"

    "Mother (he uses "Mother" in a very formal tone when he's trying to be funny) and I had this discussion earlier. How can the river be in two different places?"

    I know I'm doomed, but I respond honestly, "I don't follow you."

    He looks impatient. "That's the west coast. It can't be the Hudson."

    "Do you mean we're looking at the western bank of the river?"

    If looks could kill, I'd be dead. "Where are we, Reg?" he asks.

    "Cabrini Nursing Home, Dobbs Ferry, New York," I reply, as thoroughly as I can. He rolls his eyes, shakes his head. "Okay, you tell me where we are," I surrender.

    "We're on the west coast."

    "What state?" I ask.

    "California."

    "When did we get here?"

    "How 'am I supposed to know?" he replies.

    "What river is that?"

    "That's what I asked *you*."

I'm tempted to ask who's on first, but try logic instead. "Dad, remember when you worked on the plumbing when they were building this place?"

"Sure."

"Well, did you commute from Yonkers to California every day?" He just looks at me. "Where was the nursing home when you were working on it?"

"Right where it is now," he replies.

"And where is it now?" (I can almost taste the victory).

He points to the floor beside the wheelchair. "Right here." He smiles. I shake my head, laugh. Game, set, match.

Tuesday, February 13, 1996

Two weeks with pneumonia have taken a lot out of him. He's as weak and as tiny as he was two years earlier, just after they took the leg. He's not eating much and struggles to talk, so our conversation tonight is reduced to my yes or no questions and his slight nods. Even his ability to squeeze back when I hold his hand is gone. So many times he's been close to death, it's difficult to know (duh), to prepare yet again. His resilience has lulled us into a false sense of something that is not security – maybe eternal hopefulness. I leave him around 7:30 and spend some time at Etville with Mom, who had been with him, as usual, most of the day. Then I drive back to Norwalk.

Wednesday, February 14, 1996

Day of Hearts

I'm distributing roses and stuffed animals in homeroom as part of the Student Government's Valentine's Day celebration. Homeroom's extended because of the snow and sleet – buses are running late, and the students, even those who aren't receiving gifts, are in a maybe-we'll-get-out-early-because-of-the-snow,

Valentine's-Day type of mood. Around 8:10 Bob D'Aquila comes to my door and tells me I have phone call in the office. I know what it is immediately (he doesn't), and as I walk the ninety-second walk to the office, I wonder how to be – I wonder what it feels like when your father dies. I pick up the phone, and Becky tells me gently. She says Mom hadn't answered the home phone, and I ask her not to call her again. I'll drive there and tell her in person. I call Anne Marie, get no answer and choose not to tell her machine the news. I'll call her back.

    I leave Bob my lessons, get my coat and books, and leave the school for the drive down 95 from Stamford to Yonkers. Before I can open the front door, Mom opens it, sobbing hysterically and not knowing what to do. She had called the nursing home when she got up to remind the new shift about a change in Dad's medication, and Becky, faced with a difficult choice, chose to tell the truth, reassuring Mom that I was on my way. Our neighbor, Doris Ciufo, is already with Mom, and two minutes after I arrive, my cousin Gena, who was one of Dad's most faithful visitors, arrives.

    I shovel some snow while Gena helps Mom get ready, we drive to the nursing home and spend some time there with Uncle Frank before they move Dad from his room, and then Mom and I stop for lunch at Red Robin on Executive Boulevard. I call the funeral home to put into motion the plans we had made in January 1994, and we begin to call family and friends.

    Around 3:30 I make the drive back up 95 to my apartment in Norwalk. The snow has stopped – some three or four inches fell – I need to get the clothes I'll wear for the wake on Thursday and Friday and the funeral on Saturday. Home, I change into my running gear and drive to Calf Pasture Park, where the gates are closed, so I park outside and run in through the parking lot. No one has been here yet today – not a footprint marks the new snow, and I feel and hear the crunch of each step and relish the paradox of sweat that begins to roll down my reddening face in the chill February air. The run is good – after some forty minutes, I finish with the warm, present, relaxed feeling I've come to appreciate over twenty-five-plus years of running, and I wonder, again, how to be.

I enjoy the park's solitude – walking along the sound, trying not to think, trying hard just to be, rather than wondering how, and I find myself on the swings and feel the first chill of the sweat on my skin against the cold air. Only a few birds and squirrels see me take the swing as high as I can – almost parallel to the ground. As the chill deepens, I know it's time to go.

I return to the apartment, stretch, shower, eat, organize lessons for Thursday and Friday, make phone calls – Paul, Jerry, Alice, Tom, Laura, Rob and others – and pack my clothes. Dave Lewis, whom I've known just a few months, offers his support and comes to pick up my lessons after I offer to drop them off. I sleep and hit the road early. Thursday will be busy with the wake – non-stop visitors both afternoon and evening. Friday will bring a blizzard, offering us a day of intimate solitude at the funeral home, visited by a few hardy friends and family, and Kevin Houston's mid-storm arrival on his late afternoon drive back to Rockland from Manhattan. Saturday will be clear, cold and white. Pat Sassano will emerge from the side altar at St. Anthony's after Monsignor Robertson's homily, and deliver a soulful *Ave Maria* on his saxophone. I'll deliver the eulogy, and ask those present to celebrate 88 years of Dad's life. They give him a standing ovation. Pretty cool. Sunday I will begin the process of understanding and grieving.

❧ ❧ ❧

Later in 1996 - Undated Note

It occurs to me as I look again into what is really on my mind, in my heart and in my soul, that none of this is an interruption in our lives, although we may view it as such. None of it is a tragedy or a disaster or a shame, although we might choose to attach those labels to recent events. It occurs to me that this is, in its purest, simplest, most complex form, Life. Just the way it's "supposed to be." Not the best of all possible worlds, whatever that is; not the worst that could happen, whatever that is; not a dream come true and not even the furthest thing from our minds. It simply is what is. And the only true peace we can have in this Life, the process of healing, as Jon Kabat-Zinn tells us in *Full Catastrophe Living,* is "the process of coming to terms with things as they are."

While we are always free to reinterpret the past – give it new meaning, we are not able to change what has happened. While we are always free to work towards change in ourselves and our situations, we must be able to live this moment, as it is – not as we would have it, or as we wish it were – but simply, be it painful or pleasurable, as it is.

Another hospital stay, a professionally predicted death, a remarkable recovery, an amputation, a sudden separation from a spouse of forty-one years – less final than death, and perhaps more complex, the adjustments to life in a nursing home for both the resident and his family, the inevitable decline and death, and if we're lucky, the awareness of the dawning and dimming of each new day with its potential for learning and forgetting, for change and for staying the same, for doing and for being: all of these are ours to do with what we will. All of these are Life.

☯ ☯ ☯

February 14, 2014:

    Perhaps these journal entries, and my reflections through poetry on the dyings and deaths of my dad, mom and sister, are a subversive plot for me to remember myself, and by extension remind those who might read them to remember themselves as well. While I'm happy that I've written on family, love, loss, grief, gratitude, goofiness and gravitas, I realize that the writing is always emerging, never done. Still, here it is, and I am.

    Stephen Levine speaks in *A Year to Live* of the powerfully compassionate move in perspective from "my" pain, fear, grief, illness, etc. to "the" pain, fear, grief illness, etc. While I still experience whatever *it* happens to be, I do so within the shared human experience – it's not just *mine*, it's *everyone's*, and this is "just" my personal taste and interpretation of it. So, I've come to recognize, with each new loss, loss that is by no means exclusively mine, both the grief I hold and the grieving I've yet to embrace. I'm not sure that we ever fully finish grieving, but rather learn how to more skillfully hold it: Jack Gilbert's, "so that / he can go on without ever putting the box down."

    Because I was able, as many of us are, to 'do what had to be done' for the most part 'when it had to be done,' and I knew, at least from my neck up, that injury, illness, aging and death are 'part of the deal,' deaths of aging grandparents, aunts and uncles, while sad, seemed 'normal,' while the death of a high school classmate during our college freshman year, a cousin in her forties, and two students, Paul McDermott and Joey Ciardullo, to violent crime in 1979 and 1983 respectively, felt anything but normal. 'Normal' is no doubt an arbitrary label, but the other-than-normal losses continue to this day, and you, as you read this, know that as well. I thought I might mention here the friends and colleagues who have lost a parent, sibling, spouse or child in the past five years, but there are too many to name, and I know that doing so – honoring others – would also, ironically, be an easy out for me in this particular writing.

My Dad's last two years, depicted briefly in these poems and notes, were difficult. My Mom's last three-and-a-half years, for which I served as her primary caregiver, were difficult, but a different type of difficult. We spoke about just about everything – from the birds at the feeder to how much she missed Dad, to her own dying and death. Her health issues were real; our open, honest conversations were incredible gifts for us both. My sister Anne Marie's last six years were incredibly difficult, interspersed with bouts of happiness and hope.

I do know that while I've accepted their deaths, I also miss the hell out of them – at their, and my, respective bests and worsts. Family of origin, for good or ill, impacts us – impacts me, and yet I'm reminded of Richard Bach's words in *Illusions:* "The bond that links your true family is not one of blood, but of respect and joy in each other's life. Rarely do members of one family grow up under the same roof." I love that second sentence for the many ways I can read it, and I remind myself of my other families – Weaving Soulful Community/vision quest; Integral Coaching Canada, the remarkable Coaching and Healing group, and the larger integral community; poets, writers and teaching artists, especially, but not only, in Connecticut and New York; Sacred Heart High School, St. John's and Iona, and my monthly (in)sanity check with John, Larry, Brec and Kim, among others. And, for some fifty-five years now, Paul. Family, for sure.

And yet, I find myself in this moment resisting what I'm called to write next if I'm to bring this brief piece to an end with any level of integrity and authenticity. I spoke with Marianela last night and asked what she would be comfortable with my mentioning here, and what would be too sad to share publicly, and we reached agreement. As I continue to hold the end, at least from a flesh-and-blood perspective, of the family into which I was born, and the end, at least formally, of the family I chose with Marianela and Noé to co-create, the loss and grief, and also the love and gratitude, are palpable – and not just for me, I know. I continue to unpack, recognize and remember myself in all my beauty and blemishes, with all of the wisdom and compassion I can muster, as I'm reminded of what I think I know and what I actually embody and live moment-to-moment. Every bit of it is an opportunity to grow and live more fully.

I know that each time I believe I understand something a little more, the Mystery of what is not yet mine to understand seems to deepen. Both of these are essential – the relative understanding and the Absolute Mystery. The old lesson, again, and again.

She Rarely Let Him Finish

NEW TRICKS

My adolescent need to challenge her beliefs
long gone, we sit at the late summer table,
laughing at the birds' feeder antics, peaceful in
our ritual of my cooking, her cookies and tea for
dessert, and the comfort emerging from sugar,
caffeine, my genuine desire to see through her
eyes, and her willingness to let me have a look.

I ask what she believes, she asks, *about
what?* Everything. She smiles, I specify –
life, death, religion, politics – you know, everything.
Like, do you literally believe God created all of this
in six 24-hour days, what do you mean by heaven,
who's worse – Clinton or Starr, what are we here for,
anyway? She engages, throws questions back at me,
we wrestle with what this means for us, here and
now, and slowly, almost imperceptibly, find ourselves
in open, receptive spaciousness with room for
difference, disagreement – each other – unburdened by
expectation and desire – present, light, in this very
moment   and this   and   this.

She tells me what she believes, filtered through
warm, luminous faith, occasional showers of
doubt and the grace and openness to learn after
eight decades. We compare the Gospels with
the *Dhammapada*, Big Bang with Creation,
species evolution with individual development;
she sits in at the college, and strains with her
left ear to hear about Ken Wilber – all quadrants,
all levels – but the mutual lessons fare best in the
evening kitchen with cookies, tea and birds.

When we dare to make it real, she tells me she can't
forgive someone, we remember forgiveness releases
anger and hurt – doesn't require the other's apology –
is the best gift we can give ourselves, and she looks at
me, says, *not many people think the way you do*, as if it
were all my idea. We try it on her real-life target, learn
to differentiate theory from practice, embrace clarity and
ambiguity, forgive ourselves when we fail, and try again.

We bring up fear of death (and life), and when I ask, she
responds in calm so pure I feel it, that – no, she's
not afraid of death, in fact, she's *ready to go*.

Lesson over, dishes done, we take turns yelling at
Jeopardy and *Wheel* in the living room, laugh like
sophomores, then I work or read until it's time to
say good night – see you in the morning, and
await her inevitable tag: *God willing.*

SANITIZE YOUR PORES

Hospital sponge baths notwithstanding, five weeks have passed since her last real cleaning, and she predictably avoids the question: *I'll wait for the visiting nurse. I wouldn't want to make you uncomfortable.* Shunt insertion for dialysis was difficult. Happy to be home amid the comfort of familiar food, conversation and furniture, her left arm throbs. I suggest she's the uncomfortable one. She laughs. *You would do that? Really?* Really. When do you want to get clean? We pencil each other in after dinner. She spends ten minutes setting up, calls me in, and walks me through the clean white washcloth, shampoo, soap, towel for her feet, towel for her hair, multi-purpose towel for body parts yet to earn unique-towel status, and the gray rag for scrubbing the tub. Still in her terry-cloth robe, she says she'll do her *coomisigyam* first, then call me back. I bow, exit, wait in the hall. When I return she's sitting on the plastic chair in the tub, profile to me, turned slightly away in modesty, suggests I do her hair last so she won't get a chill, sitting with a wet head. I point out it's 85 degrees, 95% humidity in the bathroom, we laugh, but I defer to her wishes, lather up the cloth with soap and scrub her back, under her arms, her entire right arm and hand, then down both legs to her feet. She tells me to rub hard because it feels good like a massage, so I do, terrified of adding a bruise to her potato-skin-and-plum-colored limbs. She tells me to dig in with my nails as I wash her hair – thin and vibrant white against her delicate scalp. Again, I'm afraid to rub too hard, but I increase the pressure and she cheers me on – *ahh, that feels soo good.* I rinse her off with the shower massage, then step out so she can revisit and rinse her *coomisigyam,* come back, drape her with the all-purpose towel, help her lift a leg at a time over the tub wall, step carefully onto to the foot towel, and begin to dry her hair – another massage – with the hair towel. She sits on the toilet seat cover, glowing in moist warmth and next-to-Godliness. I notice the clean, white wash cloth atop the toilet tank, where it was when we began, and the gray tub-scrubbing rag hanging over the soap rack, where I placed it after using it to give her her first bath in five weeks. Oops. I feel a guilty smile emerge, realize the truth might traumatize her beyond immediate benefits of hygiene. Before I say a word, her eyes fill up, she says she *feels like a million bucks*, thanks me from the bottom of her heart, so I ask if she really feels clean. She says *beyond clean* – as good as she's felt in weeks, and I nod toward the white wash cloth on the toilet tank, ask her if that's the one she wanted me to use, and she says *yeah*, unaware that it's cleaner and drier than she is, which I point out. Silence. Then: *so what did you use?* I point to the tub scrubber, she asks if I'm serious, I say yes, observe that she's still alive, which is a good thing. She begins to laugh. *I guess I'm learning*, she says – *there was a time when this would've been a big problem.* I know, I say. I hear that Comet is real good at sanitizing your pores. We powder and deodorize; after I scrub the tub of imaginary grime she insists on putting everything away because I've done enough. Later she's in the living room, reading *The Dhammapada* in the recliner, embracing peace of mind and cleanliness. I walk in, she says she doesn't know many sons who would do that for their mothers. I say I don't know many mothers who are falling apart the way she is. She laughs. *I'm serious,* she says. *I'll never be able to thank you for all you do. I feel so lucky. Who lives better than I do?*

DIALYSIS DAYS

October: up at four-thirty – from bed to
bathroom to kitchen, washes, eats, then
slowly, button-by-button, dresses – only asks
for help when she needs it, rarely does,
then waits for the van. We walk down the
stairs together, driver takes the bag from
my hand, she wills herself up three steps,
where Dorothy waits, seated, with her
invaluable, *Good morning, Bridget.*
Dialysis partners. We wave goodbye.
I watch the van pull away.

Five hours later, I hear the engine's rumble on
the street; the instant our eyes meet I know how
she feels: on good days she takes small steps
toward me, smiles or sighs as I walk down the
driveway, take her arm and the bag; on bad
days she waits for me next to the van, eye
contact grants permission to nod her head
from side to side, hold back tears, share
the driver got lost or *I bled for half an
hour* or *I passed out again* or *I
threw up* or *I feel so nauseous.*

June: basement steps are almost impossible
after nine months, so a stair lift surprises her
when we return home after a two-week stay at
St. John's. Her first ride brings a giddiness – *it's so
smooth and quiet: who lives better than I do?*

November: she can no longer walk up the
driveway after dialysis, so I wheel her between
the van and the house each day. The dialysis

center and Para Transit debate who will wheel her
between the van and the facility. Estéban, her
favorite driver, ignores the rules and does what
needs to be done, risking his job, but even with
his love, they leave her waiting too often, and
driving her myself seems to be the way to go.

I'm exhausted, can't imagine what it's like
for her, share this with Jerry by phone one
morning, and he says, *I'll do Saturdays,* which
blows me away, not with surprise, but because I
know he means it. I fight back tears that fill me
as I try to thank him.

On November 22, she solves the problem herself
with a final late-night-emergency-room admission
that puts dialysis right down the hall.

NOVEMBER 16, 1999

She awaits eye contact before
shaking her head side to side, frozen,
still on the street after two unsteady
steps toward me. Dorothy and Estéban
look on – I take her bag, lock the chair's
wheels, gently help her off her feet,
wave to the van windshield's glare,
lower my center of gravity and push
her up the driveway. Inside the garage,
lock the wheels again, help her stand,
up one step to the basement and
stair lift. I climb first, wait for her at
the top, walk with her to the bedroom,
take her coat, hat, scarf, ask her what
she needs.

I'm so sleepy – nauseous –
I just want to get comfortable.

She walks to the living room, sits in
the recliner, I pull the footrest up, push
back near her head, slowly, the chair
shifts, she nods okay. I drape the
afghan, she cocoons, I walk to the
freezer, chip some ice in the one-cup
Pyrex pitcher, bring it to her with a
spoon – her dialysis liquid allotment.
She thanks me, says she's all set,
closes her eyes. I hang up her coat,
put the bag away, walk through the
living room on my way upstairs.
She seems to rest.

At the computer, I work with revision,
theme, texture and completion in poetry
and life, hear the recliner bang forward,
her slippers shuffle toward the bathroom. I
find her holding the lined plastic trashcan in
front of her – as softly as I can, rest my right
hand in the middle of her back, left hand on
her forehead. She heaves. *Anything?* She nods
no. Slowly settles, reclaims her breath,

I just want to go to sleep.

Back in the living room she sits up,
both feet on the floor, different
trash can ready, I kneel alongside,
she begins to sob, fights it, loses, says

*I hate to talk like this, but I've had it –
I feel so terrible that you have to go
through this, but I wish He'd just
take me – I'm ready to go.*

I envelop her in both arms, her head against my
chest, she asks if I know what day it is, I say, *yeah,
I do,* she says she tried not to think of it,
but misses him so much and fed up
with feeling so horrible, and

*I'm not trying to scare you or make you feel sad,
but I don't want to do this anymore.
I'm ready to join Dad.*

I know, I say, and hold her as sobs
settle wordlessly into spacious silence.

NOVEMBER 19, 1999

Happy 83rd!

> *Good morning – I feel as*
> *good as I've felt in weeks*
> *(knock on wood)*

We pack the wheelchair and
roll our way to a 9:30 AM
gastroenterologist at the
blue-dot building where
both-end exams find diverticulosis;

we leave prescriptions at Walgreens
then to the cemetery where from the
car   five feet from the stone
she says

> *Hello, Dad – another birthday –*
> *I hope it won't be long before*
> *I join you   Miss you*

Next, her first visit to Stew Leonard's –
not to shop, just to see – wheel our way
through the aisles – a few grapefruit? –
those pies look good – cookies for the
dialysis center on Thanksgiving? Back
to the car. Then

Red Lobster – adventurous, we leave
the wheelchair in the trunk, take
our time walking arm-in-arm –
salmon looks good – please
cook it with as little

salt as possible

Halfway through she puts her fork down

> *You know how much I appreciate*
> *all you do – this has been a great day –*

> *it still is –*

> (she laughs)   *I feel so lucky*

If you were really lucky, you'd have two working kidneys and a heart that –

> *you know what I mean – a lot of people have*
> *worse problems and no one takes care of them*

> *yeah, I know what you mean*

NOVEMBER 22, 1999

Eight-thirty, Noé's ready for bed,
Marianela tells me Mom's not okay,
I check blood pressure and pulse,
both fine, but she sits down and says,
I just don't feel right; professionals at
the drill – bag packed, medical history,
prescriptions, insurance cards, walkman
and tapes ready to go. But she's walking
around the bedroom checking everything,
I'm impatient, *if you need to go to the
emergency room, let's go; we'll take care
of this later.* Marianela shoots me a look,
I calm down, see that she's scared –
maybe for the first time. I walk her to
the living room, she sits in her recliner,
repeats, *I just don't feel right*, starts to
get up, collapses in my arms; I help her back
down, dial 911 – before I hang up I hear the
truck rumble from the Saw Mill River Road
station. Three firefighters fill the living room,
paramedic follows two minutes later. Oxygen,
history, pulse and pressure; she overhears
that St. John's ER is on diversion; responds,
I'm not going anywhere else. They look at me.
I look at her, repeat the ER is over-extended
and they're diverting patients to Yonkers General.
She looks at them: *They know me at St. John's.
Talk to the night supervisor – tell them it's Bridget
Marra, they'll take me.* They look at me again,
then at each other. The paramedic takes his cell
phone outside, comes back in, says, *You're all set
for St. John's, Mrs. Marra.* Everyone exhales. I'm not
sure he really made the call, thank him, they carry

her down the stairs, into the ambulance. I follow, see her from the ER to CCU, stay until midnight. Marianela lies awake in bed with the light on when I return. Noé sleeps. After years of doing this, each ER run brings both urgency and routine: she might not come home – immediate fear and ubiquitous reality – the volcano in the backyard.

WHAT ELSE?

520A this time
   she's sitting up
legs dangling over the
side of the bed   powdered
feet light years from
the floor
ruddy complexion against
white hair
post-Thanksgiving
smile   feeling
as well as she has in days
says the nurses told her she's
an LMP – a low-maintenance
patient – and then:
    what else did I want to tell
you   oh yeah   they got the
results of the biopsy back and it's
    cancer
then changes the subject   smiling
never missing a beat

    as if heart disease and renal
    failure are not enough

I get up from the chair   sit
next to her   put my right arm around
her   she tilts her head against me
shifts slightly   says my arm is
too heavy on her shoulder   I move it
take her left hand in both of mine
  we sit in silence

I'm so lucky to have you   she says

adds   *and we're both lucky to have Marianela*

I massage her hand gently
We kiss goodbye   *I love you   I love you too*

At the door I turn and face her
bright eyes, smiling face   *See you tomorrow*

She smiles
winks
I smile – raise index and
         middle fingers on my right hand
    intend peace, question victory
                walk out

DECEMBER 2, 1999

The room is empty when I arrive,
June Moore sees me, says Mom's in
the solarium, so I walk down the hall,
find her in the wheelchair, draped
neck down in a white blanket, facing
the window, headphones on, peaceful in
the solitude of late morning sun on the
Palisades, the river, plants and flowers
that June (with her guidance) nurtures.
I walk to her left side – she sees me,
stops Nat King Cole and we kiss hello.

I sit, we talk about the wedding, how happy she is,
how fortunate we both are to have found Marianela.
Nurses and aides remind me to get ready for our
mother-son dance, which seems as important
to them as it does to us. We laugh, hold hands,
sit in warm silence before the vast expanse of
gray river, brown cliffs, and to the south, a
miniature Manhattan's futile attempt
to reach for the deep blue winter sky.

June walks in, Mom credits her for the plants and
flowers, but June is quick to thank her for lessons
on how to bring a dying poinsettia back to life. When
she says she's tired we wheel her back to the room,
help her from the chair into bed, then slide her
gently up until body and bed become as one.

She sighs. Smiles.

Flat on her back, scars and bruises from too
many IV's, bypasses, staples, and stitches

hidden tastefully beneath crisp white sheets,
her smile transforms to laughter, then language:

Who lives better than I do?

WE ALL WANT HER

I walk from CCU
downstairs
to the lobby the day after
December 7 surgery,
meet Sandra
who
had given
Mom

*the best bath I've
had in the hospital in years*

two weeks before, and
I tell her they
removed the
tumor and
everything seems
to be going well.
All things considered,
the doctors
are amazed at
her recovery.

Sandra smiles and
says *You tell her
we all want her
back on the
fifth floor when
she gets out of
CCU – she
is so much fun
to take care of.*

WHAT DO YOU WANT TO DO?

Marianela
           finds   her
    gray and fixed-eyed   still conscious, December 14,
       Dr. Kumar asks to speak with me outside 624B – explains
       what he sees   asks

What do you want to do?

      My brain checks off years of open
conversation, health-care-proxy, DNR, recent declarations of
    readiness
to go,   and
as these thoughts almost emerge as audible sounds,
     my heart understands,
            after twenty years of miraculous recoveries, the
prospect of   her never coming home again, of
      the rapidly growing short-lived love that she and
      Marianela share, of
her prospective, palpable absence from our wedding in a month,
    of her departure's impact
on her step-grandson-to-be, Noé, whose bedroom
            shares a wall with hers, and,
     what my brain cannot process, of
       the current collision of one
    tectonic plate that wants to end her suffering and
let her rest,
     with one that wants
some more time, another meal, a good laugh, another
      visit with Jean and Jerry, and that mother-son dance
        that all the nurses are cheering for:
      one will emerge as a mountain   the other
forced below, never to be heard from again, and I –

I feel the plates squeeze down from my head, up from my
    heart
  as an academic discussion evolves into flesh-and-spirit
    reality;
what seemed   so clear   fades in the
    plate collision's dust, and too
        much blurred debris clamors   for immediate
                attention:
  What do you want
to do?   *The doctor wants to know.*
   (What do *I* want? What does *she* want?)
Finally,

   We have a DNR on file.
We've discussed this thoroughly.
                  No respirator.
   Let's just keep her comfortable.

  He accepts my words, which seem to convince us both.

    I   wait   for   him   to   say
I know how hard this is – these decisions are never
    easy; he

      silently nods and in a few minutes,
she's on her way to CCU, where we will keep
   her comfortable for twenty-one hours
      after which

   she rests in ineffable peace,
         not yet ours
      to know.

4:32 PM

Just after noon, December 15,
Anne Marie and Marianela walk
to the café for soup and coffee,
I place my right hand on Mom's
forehead, begin a Hail Mary in
her ear, she nods yes, but can't
find words until *Holy Mary,
Mother of God, pray for us sinners
now, and at the hour of our death,
Amen*, emerge as lip movement and
wispy breath. Later, four of us softly
sing Christmas carols with no response
until "Deck the Halls" allows lips and breath
one final manifest memory and
we hold on to every *Fa* and
every *La* that she
can muster, but
there aren't
many.

Three o'clock: no nods or sounds
suggest she's still with us, dopamine
and saline drips support desert horizon
palm trees and ponds. Linda checks
both human and machines, Anne Marie
sings, tells Mom again and again it's okay
to fly away, Marianela holds her hand,
hugs her, whispers in what, a few hours
earlier, was her good ear: *We're here,
mama – we're all here.*

Telemetry and recovery nurses appear,
cry for her, with us; dialysis nurses,

surrogate kidneys twelve hours a week,
partners in body and spirit, join us –
June sings, Mercy, unbelieving, wide-
and-wet-eyed, hugs us, stays, embraces
all she can of what she already misses.

Dr. Feldman reads her chart, walks out,
returns. Her cardiologist for twelve years,
he stands, back to the window, the river,
the bridge – facing her, us – eyes filling, takes
her hand, touches her forehead, suggests we
speak outside the room, review what
we all know – eyes full, overflowing,
he confirms technology's mirage,
admits the rarity of tears for him,
reviews the decade-plus relationship.
At our request Linda stops
the dopamine, leaves
the saline.

Our vision skips randomly now
from monitor's green-on-black BP
and HR readouts to her breathing body
on the bed and back again – waiting for
the numbers to confirm what we believe
we've chosen, but can never control –
perfection of her 83-year process –
and when what's measurable
measures nothing, Linda floats in silently,
a finger's touch fades
        green zeroes   to black.

The ever-present unmeasurable's screaming
    silence,
  the   breathless body before us,

>   fill the room, call us
>   to look
> once more,   at
>   who we believe she is –
>   and
>   so   we   do.

THE INGREDIENTS
- for Marianela

She arranges Vanilla Wafers, chocolate, pecans,
corn syrup, towels, wax paper, too much sugar,
rubber mallet, and bottle of rum on the table.
Wraps the bag of wafers in the towel, brings
the mallet down, gently at first – an attempt
to reduce the cookies to dust. Slowly, she
increases the blows' intensity, then rests, knowing
the large crumbs that remain must be pulverized.
She can't believe she's making Christmas rum balls
alone.

She makes her first emergency-room run
to St. John's in September, cleans, cooks,
helps her bathe – even checks to see if
that might be blood in the stool.
They laugh over dinner, share fears,
believe they'll make rum balls together.

Congestive heart failure, again—this time on the
Taconic, coming home Labor Day – dialysis, and
once more like new, they both breathe easier
until the next time   and the next and 911 three
days before Thanksgiving, rooms 416A, 420A,
510A, 509A, spin her head as the colon joins
the heart and kidneys' score-long fray within
the shrinking body, now barely able to
contain the freedom-seeking spirit.

December 7 surgery and miraculous six-day recovery:
she feeds her in the hospital, massages her feet,
rests a Reiki-powered palm against her
forehead, her chest, and they can

almost taste the rum and
chocolate.

She walks into 624B December 14, her usual smile
and *Hello, mama* ready, but gray skin, fixed eyes
and broken voice that almost greet her punch a hole
in her heart, jelly her legs, and she gets the
nurse, then phones me. Twenty hours later, bed six
in CCU, the eighty-three-old heart finally
stops beating, one month before church and
state would acknowledge us in law.

Now she wipes her eyes on rolled-up sleeves and wills
rum balls into existence. Runs out of rum and
pours brandy. Rum balls or brandy balls, she
makes love.

She always has the ingredients for that.

CHRISTMAS SPIRIT

I walk into the dialysis center December 23
with fifty one-dollar instant lottery tickets she
planned to give as Christmas gifts. Sixty-
eight hours since we buried her, sun – like me
and most of these brave souls whose blood
courses through miles of tubes and filament,
trusting technology for what nature no longer
provides – not yet up, and I get the okay to
walk patient to patient, machine to machine,
extend my hand and say, *Merry Christmas from
Bridget Marra.* Some cry. Some, who don't know,
ask how she's doing. Some, whom I haven't met,
ask if I'm her son who wrote the book. Many say
isn't this just like Bridget. One tells me of the
courage she gave him when he first came to
dialysis. A newcomer never met her, seems
confused, but thanks me. Dorothy takes my
hand, fills up, reminds me that they rode the
van together – how much she misses her. And
I remember the instructions in October: buy fifty
one-dollar instants – not all at once, but a few
at a time, different games and different agents –
better chance of getting some winners that way.
So for two months, whenever I remember, the
Odell liquor store, Hastings stationery, Central
Avenue deli, Mobil, Texaco, A&P emerge as
gift vendors for the Christmas Spirit, for the
Ghost of Christmas Present(s), and when Dorothy
lets go my hand, I give a ticket to each nurse
and near the door remember our first trip here
in November '98 – her first out-of-hospital dialysis,
machine near the window, southwest corner of
the room, and lunch at El Dorado on the way

home – I look now at rows of machines,
pulsing red tubes, busy doctor, nurses, and I
want to sever and savor this connection forever.
A nurse hands me a blue fleece blanket, wrapped in
plastic – the gift "for Bridget" that Bridget never got,
I take it, thank her, step from the building, take
an awakening breath of cold air beneath blue sky
and golden sunlight, take another breath, and
another, each, a new lesson in living without Bridget,
each a reminder, like the early-morning winter
sky and sun, the blue fleece blanket wrapped in
plastic, the leftover lottery tickets in my pocket,
of her presence, her presents, this Christmas.

THE DANCE WE ALWAYS SHARE
January 15, 2000

John and Morgan, Rob and Nicole,
Tony, Elaine and Marilyn, Jerry and
Jean, Mary and Robert,
Ricardo and Abadeza, dance
while Cliff Eberhardt's voice
and guitar fill the room,

always your face
appears in my dreams
and brings me back home tonight,

no substitute partner,
I've asked everyone to
dance, and I picture you
– lavender suit, the one
you wear forever – dancing,
smiling, holding me, fulfilling
the nurses' dreams,

always your face
in my memories
I don't feel alone tonight,

I hear your voice, what
you're saying now, and I
smile through tears that have
known a Mother's love,

no one ever warns you
how this life can toss and turn you
when you follow the paths of your dreams
how these nights feel so long

these feelings so strong
I would give anything to see you again,

ruddy complexion against white hair,
your face, not fixed and gray, but
beaming with joy at a lemon ice for
dessert – your slow dance with
liquid allocation – with joy at
a moment's pain cessation, and

the dance ends, you look up
at me, offer a kiss, and say
Who lives better than I do?
I answer, *No one, Mom,*
no one, but you fade with
the music, and Marianela is
my partner, holding me in this
mother-son dance through the
   lyric's   final   echo:
I don't feel alone tonight.

"TIDIED"

appears on virtually every page of her diary: a habit, literal and symbolic – shorthand; *tidied* – her relationships with things and people – keep them ordered, clean, presentable, or someone might think poorly of her, or worse, her family. *Tidied*, often followed by *+ Devotions; +Fed birds; +Cleaned bird droppings, etc. Tidied, J Houston called; Read paper, Bath + shampoo. Tidied + CBC profile St J +2 Wash, dry, hang, fini 11 AM. Tidied + Cooking veal stew – pressure, carrots, onions soaked potatoes – Jr supped with me; Mother's Day – AM & Jos, Jr, MM & Noé treated to dinner at Sam's DF, home – balloon fun! All left about 6pm – Good Fun! Tidied – water meter needs new ball valve; Read Dean Ornish; To zoo w Anne Marie – rented wheel chair ($20- deposit) Great Day – Great Time! Jr – CT, MM foot opr. Tidied 62 degrees crochet, foot soak meds Walgreens Rx OV Dr Packer watered sunflower OV Dr Mathew – good report pack for Put. Val. Jr – driveway – BLK TOP! Tidied haircut + iron OV Dr Mathew – dialysis 3x wk Tarrytown – left arm vry blue – Reggie*

gave me shower + shampoo! **Tidied** – *lentil soup Jean +Jerry Houston visit, 2 Beanies Carvel sorbet.*
Tidied *Sun 41*
Diverticulosis
Pericolace
Nauseous
Cemetery
Stw. Leo
<u>*REST!*</u>
Ahh!
Ahh.
Ah.
.

RESURRECTION

1.
And now I'm walking toward
the check-out at the K-Mart
on 119 & 100 – dizzy from the
move, the 4:45 AM wake-up,
too much time in the car, jobs in
Stamford and Sleepy Hollow, but
this used to be Caldor – their
favorite Caldor – lower sales tax
than Yonkers, the Pizza Deli for
lunch – and as I spot a short line
and quicken my pace, I hear the
soft Jamaican accented, *Bridget*
and I know it's for me.
I recognize the face – an aide from
St. John's – can't find her name –
Verna, she says, *Reggie*, I say –
I recognize Bridget's son, she
says, asks me how I am, tells
me she uses the prayer card mom
gave her. I say *I miss her a lot* –
she says, *Of course.* I thank her
for stopping me. For a moment
we're connected – me, to
life and love at the hospital,
Verna to a flesh-and-blood
reminder of a favorite patient,
both through a spirit that lives on.

2.
I'm climbing the stairs to
4 west – telemetry – just to say
hello. The new security guard

lets me go after I tell him I want
to thank the dialysis nurses who
cared for my mom.

Parking on Broadway, walking
through the lot to the front lobby –
familiar faces, colors, the café's
scent – a path I'd trod hundreds of
times in 20 years – most in the last
7 – this, the first not to visit mom
or dad.

I see June Moore first –
she brightens, we hug, she asks
how I'm doing, am I married – I show
her the ring. She tells me she has
the poinsettia in the closet just like
Bridget told her, then calls for Verna
and Roberta – they all say they miss her.

On 5 south, dialysis is empty,
so I ask for Mercy or June Powell
and they tell me 4 west, where
I'd just been, so I walk back
down, find no one, and begin with
7, looking both south and west on
each floor for the dialysis cart in
the hallway.

On 5 west I see a tiny, dark-haired
figure peek out from a room near
the solarium – could be Mercy –
closer, it is, we hug, she tells me
June is across the hall. I stick
my face where she can see it, and

she joins us – hugs, big smile –
says she needs to call Anne Marie
to go shopping – I give her the
number.

When I leave, it's all so familiar,
and new – not leaving someone
behind, but the cycle continues –
if not here, in Peekskill or New
Milford, Houston or Tucson,
Pearl River or the Bronx.

She Created Beauty

BUMP

The light is out in
the dark blue bedroom
with twin beds and gray
Roy Rogers bedspreads.

They hear the TV and
their parents' voices
in the living room.
Anticipatory giggles
signal the game is on.

Eleven months older she
begins with a whispered
bump, rises up under the
covers on elbows and knees,
lowers her head and
raises her butt.

Bump, he whispers back
through a gleeful grin, swings
his feet to the floor between
the beds, climbs up and sits.

They try to silence the giggles
and almost do as she shakes
the bump, then suddenly
slides her hands forward
and collapses.

He bounces once on her,
again on her bed, jumps
back beneath his covers
as laughter escapes

their noses and small
gaps in their throats.

Knock it off in there, their
father's voice thunders
from the living room. Minutes
pass, laughter subsides, they
breathe calmly again.

Bump, he whispers, rising
up with laughter on
his knees and elbows
beneath the covers.
Bump, she responds,
crosses the three-foot
chasm between their
beds, and takes her seat.
He shakes, collapses, she
bounces off and laughter
fills the room.

They are under the covers
trembling and red-faced
with almost-stifled laughter
and failing feigned sleep
when their father appears.

That's enough, he says. *I don't
want to hear another peep from
you two tonight.*

They hear his footsteps
creak the wooden hallway
floor and disappear in the

the living room carpet.
An eternal moment passes.

Peep.
      Peep.

The giggles begin again.

(SOME OF) HER OWN WORDS

Her thesis, *QuiltSongs,*
Ulterior Motifs & the
Spine of Creativity:
Patchwork Stories, Meaning
Making & Metaphor:

I'm an intuitive, non-rational,
nonlinear thinker   who
favors asymmetry
    in patterns   and
landscaping,   random
harmony in song, and

the   unexpected
                  in
      general. I

thrive on   improvisation.

Student   musician   singer
    painter   quilter   poet   Scrabble-
 player   party   host   persona rubs
up against spouse, daughter, sister, friend,
administrative assistant shadow who yearns
for straight, fresh asphalt and double yellow
lines, within which creativity flourishes and
improvised, asymmetrical meaning is made.

CREATION CONTINUES

with each twig the jay
brings to the nest,
gentle raindrop,
final autumn's leaf,
Facebook friend and
miraculous snowflake,
creation continues

with every thought,
gesture, word, and
bank bailout, each
stitch sewn and
metaphor imagined
with each breath
including your last
creation continues

with every devastation,
flood, cremation,
burial, divorce, hurricane,
bullet and birth
creation continues

with every pre-emptive
strike and rainbow's
promise, state execution
and sound bite creation
continues with every

reporter uttering Wall
and Main, each family of
flora, fauna and organized
crime, and every complete

rotation misnamed a
sunrise or set creation
continues.

It is big, and beyond a bang
more a Biiiiiiiiig Baaaaaaaaaaaaaang…
still emerging this moment   and this…

It is You, beyond you
and includes you.
You have a role to play.
It is uniquely yours.

REMEMBERING IS PREFERABLE

Some never remember.
They believe they were
created but never create
themselves. Refuse
the creator's role. Not
a grandiose refusal to
create weather or
obedient children, but
the simple act of
bringing into existence
something beautiful or
authentically ugly in the
eye of a beholder.

Some remember
one thing that
flows relentless and
focused from them as
a quilt, song, painting,
poem or new or effective
way to see truth or do good.
Fame often claims them.

Others remember a lot in
a scattered way and create
quilts, songs, paintings
poems and new and
effective ways to see
and do a lot. We hear
less about them.

PLEASE DON'T ABANDON ME

She makes the phone request unsteadily
aware she's stuck and stationary two
years after the divorce, feels impatience
juxtaposed with my genuine support.
Misguided rebound relationship ends
ugly, compounds the seventeen-year loss,
pillcohol cocktails damage head and car,
embarrassed, scared and hurt she tries again.
Po' ho's performance poetry helps her
slam depression eighteen months until a
second rebound gets away, leaving her
defenseless and blind to any exit.
Too sad to talk, she texts, I drive fifty-
two familiar miles to Hiawatha Road.

STILL ON THE BED

Sometime after three, I
park in the driveway
behind the silver Rav 4
with the *Creative People
Must Be Stopped* bumper
sticker in the rear window.

I knock, wait, knock,
wait, minutes pass,
I use the keys, unlock
both locks, step
inside, announce
myself in the kitchen

follow the hallway
to the left and my
line of sight widens to
the bedroom, her body
appears still on the bed,
head tilted slightly left,
left arm extended, bent
knees lean right, feet
together to the left as
if she's stretching her
lower back. Multicolored
fleece top rides up
above her distended
belly, clashes with the
patchwork quilt below
her feet.

Two rivulets of dried
translucent purplish

fluid remain
where they flowed
briefly from her left
nostril and the corner
of her mouth.

I touch her foot, her
forehead, ask what
she's done, speak to
her, pray briefly, call her
Anne Marie. Call nine-
one-one. And wait
four hours
functionally numb with
paramedic, trooper and
detectives, answering
questions on meds, divorce,
ex-husband, ex-housemate,
last contact in response
to my voice- and e-mail
inquiries into how she is

her 3.11.09   11:10
AM text *Ok.*

Priest, eulogist, poet,
brother, I speak
as if I know
of impermanence, life and
death to friends and family,

begin a paper search
because I must

call legal, bank and retail

strangers, lose, gain and
surrender control, learn
nothing begins or ends
well with Wells Fargo
and choose mindful
conversation practice when
bank executive slaughter
begins to seem ethical.

Her house regresses to a
commodity, sells in eight
months, my garage fills
slowly again as I allow
money law and stuff
to distract me from
my grief.

THE SNIPER

breathes deep,
slow,
squints through the
scope,
    truth
in the cross-hairs,
    the solution,
precisely committed
to freeing the hostage.

Last resort,
attainable horizon, not
a solution, but
    the

solution when
negotiation or
hard work   fails
or   takes
 too
     long.

If only it were that easy,
held hostage as we are –
bliss and rage, reason
and myth,
memory,
all of them,
always them, without
which
we might see
clearly
find freedom.

Who was the sniper
for the pain
that held you hostage?

What did she see,
or not, through
that narrow scope
before she squeezed the
trigger –

another option
perhaps, just outside
her field of view,
a hair away from
your final
solution.

We all
play each role –
taker, hostage, sniper –
moment-to-moment holding,
held, setting free.

Problem and solution.

We love the scope
the crosshair's promise,
at   times
    too   slow,
or quick to squeeze
the trigger,

        release
the solution's
allure and
terror.

AWAITING THE JUDGES

Ersatz idols
deliver masterpieces
finally or every day, bring
tears and wide eyes to
the audience, already
on their feet, and wait –
Paul, in fear,
Susan, confused,
struts off stage then
returns to learn what
everyone knows.

After the voice passes through
and emerges from them
they await the judges' verdicts,
seem not to know who they are
and what they have done,
like us, look outside for approval,
despite the voice, the song,
the words, the colors,
the beauty and
breath that bring
each of us alive.

But when Evan skates
for gold, finishes
his program, still on the
ice eternal minutes
before the judges'
quantified opinions,
he vibrates – present,
celebratory – knowing
what he has done and

who he is, needing no one
to confer value, and

when asked, not
about medal, success
or program, but
Possibility and belief in
himself, without pause
he responds *It takes so much
hard work to really believe it.*

THIRTEEN WAYS OF LOOKING AT WELLS FARGO

I
Among countless subprime lenders,
the only valid thing is
oh – nothing is valid.

II
I am one of millions of
taxpayers not in default
who have to help
bail out Wells Fargo.

III
Wells Fargo survives and
gives bonuses to executives.
My sister receives no bonus
or bailout. She takes too
much Cardizem and dies.

IV
The people and the government are one.
In a democratic republic kind of way.
Sort of.
The people and Wells Fargo are not one.
Fuck Wells Fargo.

V
I do not know
which to prefer, the
Wells Fargo I helped save,
or the Wells Fargo I encountered

when my sister died.
Preferring neither seems
the way to go.

VI
Tourists write policies
followed by obedient
cubicle-dwelling masses
adorned in headsets
answering 1-800 numbers
keeping shoddy records.
I repeat every detail every
time with someone
different.

VII
Oh, Wells Fargo
executives in Malibu,
why do you imagine
you can party in a
foreclosed home?

VIII
Jessica, the computerized woman,
calls me more than fifty times.
She stalks me by phone.
I would like to virally violate Jessica,
and the virtual stage coach she rides in on.

IX
I ask Josh, a live,

innocuously helpful
headset-adorned
cubicle dweller,
if I may speak with Jessica,
he tries not to laugh, but does.

I tell him I prefer
anesthesia-free root canal
to dealing with Wells Fargo,
he again fails in his attempt
not to laugh.
I tell him laughter is okay;
the root canal is hyperbole.
Unlike my criticism.

X
Josh's supervisor tells him
the court papers I fax are
unacceptable since they
arrive without the raised seal.
I check the calendar, but it's
late August, not April 1.
The supervisor is serious.

To his credit,
Josh prefaces the news with
*You're probably not going to like
what my supervisor just told me.*
Josh is right.

XI
I ask Josh to inform

his supervisor that a fax
transmits two dimensions
– length and width – not depth.
Before he asks, I tell him
I've set the scanner to dark,
but the raised seal casts no shadow.

The raised seal is barely raised,
shallow, perhaps anemic, yet healthy
contrasted with Wells Fargo.

XII
Months pass after my sister dies.
Winter fades into
Spring fades into
Summer is about to end.
Everything changes except one thing.
Wells Fargo stays the same.
Wells Fargo sucks.
Rain Man left that out.

XIII
Wells Fargo sucks so badly
that thirteen ways of looking
will not suffice.

Wells Fargo deserves more –
31 flavors? 57 varieties?
Yes, the post-thirteen-ways,
thirty-one flavors of Wells Fargo.

FLAVOR I
This is Jessica from Wells Fargo Home Mortgage,
calling in regard to your mortgage.
Please call us back at 866-228-3535.

Our business hours are 7AM to 10 PM Central Time Monday
through Friday and 8AM to 2PM Central Time on Saturdays.
To allow us to better assist you, please have your loan number
available. Again, the phone number here is 866-228-3535.
Then kew.

FLAVOR II
On May 5 I find a ½" by 8 ½" strip of paper
stuck inside my sister's storm door. It reads:

Our representatives called on you today
while you were out.
There is an important matter
that we would like to discuss with you.
Someone from Wells Fargo leaves this
at my dead sister's vacant home
45 days after they learn of her death.

FLAVOR III
On June 2, Mr. Rogazo from Wells Fargo calls
then says he can't continue the conversation
until I have court papers appointing me executor.
I mention that he called me,
which seems not to faze him.

FLAVOR IV
On June 4 Judy from Wells Fargo calls

and I tell her she can't continue the conversation
until I have court appointment papers.
She agrees. We chat briefly about death and dying.
I hope they don't fire her for this. I like Judy.
She seems, well, human.

FLAVOR V
On July 2 JD, Wells Fargo employee # 655 calls.
I ask if he knows Mr. Rogazo or Judy.
He doesn't, but reads their notes.
I tell him what I told them.
He agrees.
I ask him why they keep calling
to tell me they can't talk to me yet.
He doesn't know (or isn't saying).
He offers to send a cease and desist order
to stop the *we-can't-talk-to-you-yet* calls.
I accept.

FLAVOR VI
On July 7 a not-Jessica,
unnamed computer
from Wells Fargo calls.
I neither pick up nor return the call.
No computer is going to tell me it can't talk to me yet.

FLAVOR VII
On July 9 the not-Jessica computer tries again,
and again, I prevail.

FLAVOR VIII
Wells Fargo and Wachovia are one.

Wells Farchovia.
W is a bad omen
as a middle initial or
the first letter of a bank's name.

In addition to notifying them
by phone and mail,
I sit with a Wachovia Bank vice-president
in her office on July 16,
hand her an original death certificate
and she makes a copy of the executor papers.
I tell her that the credit card and equity line
will be paid when the house sells.
We close my sister's checking account
and open an estate account.
Had I known
how the ensuing months would unfold,
I would have opened these accounts
with my distant cousin, Vito,
who in his own way is a banker of sorts,
if you know what I mean.

FLAVOR IX
Because I cannot find the key,
on July 18 I return to the Wachovia branch
and pay $150 to drill out my sister's safe deposit box,
which is, of course, empty.

FLAVOR X
On July 22 Daniel from Wells Fargo calls,
and I pick up.
I'm an idiot.

But we're almost even since he's an asshole,
and we engage in full frontal assault.

I ask him if Wells Fargo is recording the conversation
for quality control purposes, he says yes,
and I tell him I'm recording too,
which upsets him.
He says it's against the law,
and I ask where,
in the former Soviet Union?

We don't reach any kind of agreement.
I wasn't recording the call,
and wonder what's worse,
an illegal recording or lying about one.

Then I remember I don't care
because Wells Fargo sucks.

FLAVOR XI
On July 25, I call Wells Fargo
to see if they have received
the court papers I faxed,
but I call too late and no one answers.
A good call.

FLAVOR XII
On August 3 a process server
delivers a Wells Fargo foreclosure summons
to my cousin in North Carolina.
She is not an executor.

FLAVOR XIII
On August 7 at 9PM
a young man from Wachovia bank
calls from Florida
asking to speak with my sister
because her equity line is overdue.
I am concise
and more or less kind with him.

FLAVOR XIV
On August 18 John from Wells Fargo
tells me he cannot find the death certificate
or court papers in the files.
I refax them and call back
but he says it takes 3-4 days
for them to get into the system.
I ask him for a street address,
and mail copies as well.

FLAVOR XV
On August 20 Mr. Harrison from Wachovia bank
calls to let me know that my sister's accounts are delinquent.
I direct him to the vice-president with whom I'd met.
He has no record of my dealing with her.
I remember that Wells Fargo and Wachovia are one.

FLAVOR XVI
On August 21, a U.S. Marshall
delivers a foreclosure summons
to my front door.
I tell him I've been waiting for him

since they served my cousin
in North Carolina 18 days earlier.
He seems not to have a sense of humor.

This is also the day
I have my raised-seal conversation with Josh
(see the Tenth Way of Looking, above).
Josh suggests I bring the unacceptably faxed,
anemic-seal documents to a local Wells Fargo
branch, which he doesn't realize is almost
an hour away. I'm tempted to ask if he's seen
Dog Day Afternoon or *Harley Davidson
and the Marlboro Man*, but realize I could
get in trouble for joking about something
like that because banks are important
and people are not.
I simply respond,
*Josh, I appreciate your attempts to help,
but that's just not gonna' happen.*

FLAVOR XVII
On August 25 at 8:38 AM
someone from Wells Fargo calls,
I pick up, and no one is on the line.

FLAVOR XVIII
On August 29 I receive an unsigned letter
from Wells Fargo thanking me
for talking with them. I believe
it refers to the Josh conversation,
but it isn't clear. They *value* me

as a customer and *realize this
may be a difficult time* for me.

FLAVOR XIX
On August 31 I receive a letter
from Wells Fargo dated August 26.
It is *in response to the notification
of the death of the mortgagor on the
loan referenced above* and they want
me to *please accept* their *sincere condolences
for* my *loss.*
The name *Betty Shank* appears
at the bottom of the letter without a signature.
And the stage coach she rides in on as well.

FLAVOR XX
On September 8 I receive eight copies
of the same letter from Wachovia,
four via Certified Mail; two addressed
to my sister's married name; two
addressed to her maiden name;
two addressed to her estate using
her married name and two addressed
to her estate using her maiden name.
All are mailed to the address at which
she lived and died and forwarded
to me at the address at which
she never lived and I've not yet died.

FLAVOR XXI
On September 12, the not-Jessica
Wells Fargo computer calls again.

I call back and speak with a very
young-sounding Marlen, who
looks at the notes and tells me
the court papers never made it
into the system until recently.
She gives me a number for
Wells Fargo liquidation services
but knows nothing about the
foreclosure process.
She seems like a good kid,
and polite, but *Holy Shit.*

FLAVOR XXII
On October 2 my attorney tells me
that Wells Fargo requires 7-10 business days
to issue the pay-off letter she has requested
for the imminent sale of my sister's house.
Imminent is my word.

FLAVOR XXIII
On October 13 John from Wells Fargo calls
(why do I pick up?). He knows nothing
about the sale of the house or the payoff letter.
I try to engage him in conversation
about customer service, and my experience
with his bank. He responds that
banks the size of Wells Fargo
just can't provide the level
of customer service you're suggesting.
I let his words hover in sustained silence,
then say, *That's exactly my point.*

He appears not to have heard either of us
and asks if there's anything else
he can help me with today.

I remind him that he called me
and that he hasn't helped me
with anything today,
except to confirm that
Wells Fargo is too big
to provide quality
customer service.

He tells me to have a great day.
After we hang up, I string together
one of the most creative combinations
of profanity I've ever heard or uttered
and feel both good and bad when I finish.
Mostly good.

Flavor XXIV
On October 19 Jessica,
the computerized Wells Fargo phone rep
quoted in Flavor One, calls.
She will call almost every day until November 9.

Flavor XXV
On November 3 we close on
the sale of my sister's house.
The foreclosing attorney
introduces himself as the
buyer's attorney, but I
remember his firm's name

from the summons. He steals
$845.00 in foreclosure fees
from the sale although we were
never close to foreclosure.
Fuck him, his beady little eyes,
his attempt to appear casual,
bright and articulate at the table,
and his tweed jacket too.
I will see him in hell.

Flavor XXVI
When I arrive home after the closing,
Carolyn, an apparently not-computer-
generated woman from Wells Fargo,
has left a message for me.
I don't call back.
I now have nothing to lose, and
I know what I'm capable of.
I'm worried about Jessica though.
What have they done with her?

Flavor XXVII
On November 7, Jessica calls.
I'm glad she's okay.

Flavor XXVIII
On November 9 Jessica calls again.
Back to her old tricks.
I don't know it at the time, but
this is the last time she'll call.
She pronounces *thank you* as if

if it were spelled *then kew*,
and I'll miss that.

Flavor XXIX
On November 13, Wells Fargo
congratulates me on
paying the loan in full.
They are *pleased to have been of service*
... and would welcome the opportunity
to provide future financing solutions.
I'm looking for the fine print
where they mention that
icebergs thrive in hell and
that they are a company of happy,
misguided idiots, but I don't find it.

Flavor XXX
On November 27 Wells Fargo sends a letter
to inform me that my loan has met one of the following
conditions: *paid in full; transferred to another mortgage*
company, loan assumed, or the escrow account was deleted.
Does this mean they're not sure?

Flavor XXXI
Wells Fargo and Wachovia are one.
In my best moments I am one with everything.
I am not one with Wells Fargo or Wachovia.
I am zero to them.
I realize that thirteen ways of looking,
even with thirty-one flavors, are not enough.

A Final Way of Looking at the Flavors of Wells Farchovia
It is only about the money.
It is always about the money.
And it is going to be about the money.
All's well that ends Wells Fargo well.

Disclaimer
That final line in *A Final Way of Looking* above constitutes wordplay loosely based on the title of a Shakespearan play and should not be construed as a threat against any bank, water source or city in North Dakota. No bean-counters, bankers or customer service representatives were injured or killed during the writing of this poem, although many deserve a good thrashing.

A Post-Final Wayvor
On June 14, 2011, two years and three
months less three days after her death
I receive letters addressed to my sister
from both Wachovia and Wells Fargo
reminding her that she still has access
to her equity line of credit, and that all
future correspondence will arrive under
the Wells Fargo logo.

Just when I thought I was out,
they pull me back in.

FIVE YEARS LATER

The tv sergeant reassures
the officer who bemoans
the imperfect but not
lethal ending, thinking
she hadn't done enough,
that indeed she had done
all she could, more than
enough, and the thought
emerges again as if
    for the first
        time,
what if I arrived earlier or
the day before, or if I'd not
been conditioned by her past
behavior, numbed to yet
another trip to see if she
were all right, which she
always was. Sort of.

And then:
it doesn't matter
how many times
I get it right,
am there on time,
every time, all the time,
the only one that matters
is the one too late,
the imperfect one,
the counter-terrorist reminder.
We only know and care about
the one they don't stop.
Not the ones they do.

Somewhere Wisdom says this
one too is perfect –
a final perfection perhaps

and Compassion holds me, tells
Wisdom to shut the fuck up
while nodding in agreement.
So I embrace them both.

And then another thought.

And Now, Still

AND NOW, STILL

1.
old photographs evoke memory and
imagination as if different

Images captured ten years before me
reveal a young man I never knew,
finding himself in Norfolk, on Tawara,
Tinian and Saipan – a young man with
fifty-one years to go, balancing
rifle, wrench and typewriter
      unaware of the woman with whom
he'll share forty-four years and
oblivious to the children they'll have,
the house on Etville, unborn
nurses who will fall in love with them,
      unconcerned with amputation,
bypass and dialysis
they will one day credit
for bittersweet longevity.

Images captured ten years before
me reveal a young woman I never
knew, searching for herself in Canada,
Italy, Hunter College, the Riverdale estate
where her father took care – a
young woman with fifty-five years to go,
    teaching first-graders
      unaware the man she will meet
and marry stands in Pacific harm's way,
too short to serve in three and tall enough
on his fourth attempt to enlist at Whitehall
Street in post-Pearl Harbor New York.

.

Images captured nineteen
years after me reveal a
sister I often understood,
long, straight, dark brown
hair, multi-colored halter top,
faded jeans and bare feet,
clear eyes filled with possibility,
music, color, texture, and shape
on her own between nuclear
limits and freedom's burden,
unaware the man she will
meet, marry and come to hate
enters early adolescence, each
oblivious to the home, betrayal and
unkindness they will share without
a parent's stability after her mother dies.

2.
I see him at eighty, dunking Stella
D'oro breakfast treats, feigning
surprise with each mushy clump
that falls into the coffee
then working the garden,
taking a break beneath the
maple tree in the metal chair,
a long slow drag on his only vice,
flicking it away and back to work.

With too much space and silence I remember
clattering Yahtzee dice on kitchen table, recliner's
bang returning upright, theme from *NYPD Blue*,
slippers shuffling across hardwood floors, faint, even
stair-lift hum, and back-door view of birds
battling for breakfast around the
feeder that hangs still from

the clothesline.

I hear the clear-eyed voice embracing Joni,
Joan, Janis and Judy, *Red Rubber Ball*
and parental *You Are My Sunshine*
requests, now silent, and

I see each epitaph, newly cut into
stone, inches from his
       He could spin a yarn
her chosen response –
       She rarely let him finish and
my choice for the daughter who
joined them too early,
    Bump partner sister,
      She created beauty
and I know the truth in each.

When they engrave
February 14, 1996
   December 15, 1999
     March 17, 2009
I feel etched stone's
temporary permanence,
time, laughter, conversation,
and wedding-day-dance
might-have-beens –
what always already is
screaming, spacious silence,
first and final truth, lost shinanklefoot,
conjured cigarettes, twilight lobby window
waves, ruddy complexion against white hair,
dialysis filters tinted pink by tired blood,
green zeroes fading to black, another knock
with no response, two key turns, a silent sister

on a loveless bed in a sad room in a lonely house
trying to remember who we are
   in order to say
       Who lives better than we do?
and mean it.

NUCLEAR FAMILY

Reversals
render my
nuclear family
unclear
and nucular families
everywhere
uncular.

My core is hollow,
my reactor shut down,
my nuclear family
once clear, then
unclear, now gone.

I don't believe a
clean-coal family
that could be
mine exists.

The wind-powered
family I meet
scatters in the
breeze when
blowhard neighbors
propelled by concerns
with appearances
complain.

The solar family's
bureaucratic panels
require my wearing
70 SPF 24/7
to avoid losing

another chunk of me to
basal cell carcinoma.

Sadly   old-fashioned
as they are, the
hydroelectric family
doesn't give a dam.

My nuclear family is gone
and at my core I am still
unclear how to react.

WRITING AGAIN
- *for Marianela, February 14, 2008*

She's writing again –
this time as I drive
the car.   She
remembers a scent or
feeling from childhood and
embodies it   writes
quickly, never seeks   but
feels and thinks   metaphor,
sees the world
       through
something else – sees
each thing   through
another.

Do I have a napkin
in the car?   No. She
finds a map
       scribbles in the margins
determined not to lose
what clamors
to be heard and seen
on the page, as I'm
determined to find the map
legible next time I need it.

She's writing   again.

Twenty-first Century
consciousness conjuring
images of pre-Columbus
Taínas celebrating
themselves   before Eve's

story   reached   their
        shores
before the snake
before the gravity
of Newton's   fallen
               apple.
Her father orders *jamón*
y queso   *jamón y*
     queso
and her language
dances across the page
     her voice   alive in English
thrives   *en el español*

and as I listen, I
remember the tear-stained
mallet pulverizing Vanilla
Wafers   as alone as   the
oh-no after the knife
escaped the cheese and
found the soft flesh
between   her   fingers, the
muffled thump of the fall
on carpeted steps and
uncertainty's

momentary
   eternity.

I remember all of
it and I want her to live
forever
       to see and taste
the emergent ripening of her tropical
soul, this

        breathing poem   this
woman   I   love.

She's writing again and
as the words dance she
sits perfectly   being
who she always already is.

She writes.

SURPRISED BY GRIEF

inevitably hard nuclear
family death darkness
pales in light of
the kitchen clock's
relentless reminders audible
throughout the house

amid *la Taína's* palpable
living absence

la poeta

persistently shared
her desire to die first
to avoid missing
me, now still
breathing leaves
space I don't want
silence too loud and
the hole in my heart's
the whole of my heart

no way we
walk away
from this love without
heroic
effort and

yet we do

with our respective
individual

true and partial
heroisms

two, but
not of a kind

different hands

we fold.

NURSING HOME RETURN
- for Joanie and Shirley

She sits on the veranda
late evening sun
above the Palisades
deepens the soft warm
radiance of her face.

Massaging the swollen left
hand in both of hers
she alternates between
drill sergeant and dutiful
loving daughter
demanding and deferential
always a quick smile ready.

The nursing home conjures
my memories of many wheels
in motion sitting down
and as I watch her love
the hand that held and
loved her earliest moments
the certain uncertainty of
life loss and love surrounds
scares and supports us.

THE RICKETY BRIDGE
- for Joanie

Heart aroused
I walk across
the rickety bridge
above the roaring gorge,
fear falling, collapse
exhaustion and
attribute
perhaps
my aroused heart
to the woman standing
on solid ground where
the bridge ends,
beyond which I
neither see nor know
anything. She invites
and resists my approach.

I stand on shaky ground
and watch him walk
across the rickety bridge
toward me in a fog
of difficulty behind, within
and looming below. He
misattributes his aroused
heart to me, mistakes me
and my ground as solid,
unaware what's behind and
within me. He gets steadily
closer, my own heart
aroused, anxious
from a patterned path
perhaps

I yearn for the hand
he offers
alluring danger,
frightening safety,
open heart.

Amid one Story and billions of stories
one man crosses a rickety bridge
toward a woman who waits
on the other side.
He attributes his aroused heart
to her. She's not so sure.
How each responds as he
approaches determines
and is determined by
what they do next. They
love and fear, have
complete and no control.
They choose and are chosen.
Each moment is theirs,
holds and is
everything.

THE WOUND

The wound and
pain are given
and old

you choose
your
suffering

when you feel
the itch, pick
the scab

feel the itch
pick the
scab

a pattern

you
choose

to keep it fresh,
raw, open,
visible

keep the
past present
wound in focus

whose fault you think
and how unfair
it was, it is

pain, universal
suffering,
uniquely yours

how many
cycles do
you require

familiar itch, tightening
skin, healing scab,
you pick

unable
to let go
you pick

you
choose
and pick

the wound and
pain are given
and old

you choose
your
suffering.

WHEN I MAKE MYSELF SMALL

When missing coins
newer clothes and cars
finer wines
wonderful workshops
alluring eyes
prospective or even
present promise
pleasure or pain
define me
my vision narrows
I feel small and can
no longer lose or risk
losing what leaves
or what I love and still
live and love fully.

Within my small embrace
fear fills the little bit of
me that's left. *I'm not
good enough* and
*how could you
do this to me*
become useful
meaningful or
even true.

When I make
myself small
the world and you
are small and
our separate smallness
blends and blames
until it becomes us

and all there is.

How much smallness in
this infinite unfolding is
mine
    yours
        ours
            theirs?

Interesting questions
and irrelevant.

Time to let go.

First Family

FILLET OF SOUL WITH A DARK NIGHT GLAZE
- for Kris Kristofferson and Ken Wilber

Endless, empty darkness,
ineffable, voiceless eternity,
no   thing   to speak of

just   this

Still
         Perfect
                 Silence

now

light so bright it
hurts your hair
since you're there to see
it and
the good news is you
both see and be it
since you are it

in this manifest
game of Absolute
hide and seek

suddenly
infinitely empty void
fills with potential
for – well, everything,
expanding in all
directions and no direction
but forward –

an omni-directional
vast, silent explosion
into and as infinity

timeless, ever-present
Awareness – oh my, God –
you choose to manifest,
hurtle through hot
endless nothingness,
slow, cool, begin to
take form –
liquefy, solidify,
learn to breathe

and you're still learning
       with   this   breath

emerging neural cord
begets slithering impulse,
    begets hairy emotion,
        begets operational thought,
gets more and more complex,
even now –

and look at you, becoming us,
Mr. and Miss *Homo habilis*
with our opposable thumbs,
creating tools with which
we attempt to grasp
the ungraspable, and

Mr. and Mrs. *Homo erectus*
standing upright on both twos,
recognizing our connection
with each other, learning

to simmer those early grunts and
calls into language that helps us
find our voice and endeavor
to speak the unspeakable, and

embrace the dawning
human potential movement
sending us in search of
warmth, and that first
success-driven speech, a
short, truncated vowel
accented by an index finger
pointing toward
the cave – *uh*   and

Mr. and Ms. *Homo sapiens*
start to share big stories as
myth emerges from magic
and calls forth reason –
Copernicus, Bruno, Kepler
and Galileo tag team
a parade of pontiffs –
Bruno gets a stake and fries
    that Clement Eight, Galileo suffers
Urban renewal – together launch
the science-religion smackdown,
and the winner is
       to be announced
during intermission at the Apocalypse
Theater's infinite showing of the
Eternal Present –
      unwrapped
beneath the bodhi tree, on the cross and
mountaintop, in the cave – or
    wherever you happen to find your Self.

Check the Universal Nondual News
for show times

right now, look to the lofty,
shaved-head, everyone-is-right,
tetra-arising, talking-horse's-
human part of you – *oh, Wilber* –
Spirit-in-Action by any other name
is still
        a rose   arisen
    a   raisin' as the Sun
from this waking dream to

face the challenge of lying
in the luxury of multiple perspectives,
creature comforts   and   I - Am - ness

while the prosthesis business
booms in Baghdad,
Bethesda   and beyond

        rest in the timeless
perfection of this very moment

while the hole in your heart
blossoms   too big to   bear,
    too intimate to bare

and the move from
me   and   you
    to us
        to all of us
to all that is   is   just this,

    just   this,   but

sometimes so hard to remember,
to shift   to move on

and we don't know in that moment
when the sheep leaves his fold
when the fool flees her flock

if he's a rebel without a clue, she's
of little faith, or the next emerging
evolutionary perspective –

what's a shepherd to do?

As I speak, whose voice
is this, really – whose vision
informs my first-person pronoun –
the eye of flesh? the eye of mind?
the I of Spirit? Or, perhaps,
the Cistercian's anonymous
authority of the collectivity
speaking through yet another
case of mistaken identity?

Inquiring minds want to know.

I am in this room, and
I am this room and
everything and everyone
in it.   I am music,
silence and
of course   I love myself
and every   single   one of me

whom I'm nevertheless called to ask –
do I authentically transcend

and include the
skin-pigmentation thing, the
masculine-feminine thing, the
hetero- homo- trans-
and bi- thing, those
ever-resilient ethnic and
religious things, the
liberal-conservative,
wisdom-compassion,
justice-mercy, and
intimacy-solitude things, and
      can I finally stop seeking
what's impossible to avoid

what I always already am

and fully feel my
absolute Embrace, my
Mother of all diversity issues,
the One as the Many,
who invites me to sit down in
the One Taste restaurant,
order my fill
from the Emptiness menu

*– I've already had the Fillet of Soul
with a Dark Night glaze, so bring
me whatever you prefer –*

dine alone with you, with us,
with all of us, in the company of
all that arises moment-to-
moment in ever-present
Awareness, savoring every
morsel of each course served

   in this Nondual Feast

still desire,
   have room for
     and enjoy
the sinfully divine, moist
midnight chocolate cake,
get up from the table
  wash all the dishes
    return to the street, and
in my own voice
  eternally
nourish and nurture
  all sentient beings?

———

Excerpt from a January 24, 2007 email from someone I didn't know:

"Reggie, I don't believe we've actually met but anyone whose poetry is endorsed by Naomi Shihab Nye and who works with Ken Wilber has GOT to have something big going for him!

"....it is just a fledgling idea I'm exploring at the moment. I'm designing the NSA Convention this July in San Diego. I'm going to get our crowd to a higher level of consciousness or die in the attempt! This program will have a very strong neuroscience / metaphysical undercurrent to it and I'm planning to disrupt pretty well every dimension of the Convention that I can get my hands on in order to get people thinking differently.

"Poetry and music, I think, are the two best channels to a higher zone. I'm looking for someone who will wax poetic about full human potential / the integral world / creating reality etc. in the opening night of the Convention, July 9. Would you feel good about doing something like that and would you be willing to if I can set it up?"

Thanks to Ian Percy, who had me at "disrupt," for knowing who Naomi and Ken are, and for the invitation, which I accepted, and which led to my writing "Fillet of Soul With a Dark Night Glaze," which I presented to some 1,200 folks who weren't in San Diego to hear poetry. No one got hurt.

FREEDOM
(April 24, St. Johnsbury, VT)

With nothing left to lose
some thirty-five years later
I thank Kristofferson
and shake his hand Sunday night –
show him the arts
and entertainment section
with his photo above mine.
Have the opportunity
to pose for the camera later,
but watch his eyes
each time he gathers himself
for another flash
with another stranger
who wants a tangible memory,
and I feel his raised eyebrows
and inhale each sigh he exhales
each time a new face approaches.
I recognize my own discomfort
in adding to his
and know a photo isn't what I want anyway.
Rather, a simple conversation,
sustained eye contact
to reveal that moment –
I was sixteen
when the morning burned golden
on the mountain in the skies
and opened my eyes
to a place in my soul

I'd not known before.
When the fiction writing
football playing Blake quoting
Golden Gloves boxer Rhodes Scholar
Army Ranger Captain janitor actor
singer songwriter poet loomed larger than life
and screamed a terrifying, exhilarating *Possibility*
that still echoes in my ears today.
Back then I thought it was about him
but now I know it's about me.
About duty. About my own voice.
The photograph would be nice to show people.
Better I stay hungry
and see what Possibility has in store for me
with this next breath and
another word for nothing left to lose.

YOU STOOD UP

So you stood up
and no one got hurt

not even you –
little you, that is,
since Big You can't
be hurt – and some,
including you, got
better, or bigger, or
more deeply authentic,
or realized

they could get better
or bigger, or more
deeply authentic and
that's a start.

So you stood up
and got better and
bigger and no one
got hurt. You opened

your mouth and they
listened. You opened
your ears and you heard.

You opened your eyes
and everything you
saw opened your
heart as well, and

your open heart
exposed the mask

of fear your mind
mistook for you,

so you stood up
and no one got hurt.

KNOWING

Now that you know
you awake to immense
freedom every morning

No going back to
real or imagined
restraints of earlier times

Nothing in the way now
save streaming limitations
in small memories of imagined

shortcomings never invited
but always completely at home
in the mind's undisciplined moments

Now that you know
you know knowing
is not enough

Squirrel at first light doesn't
know it can jump to the
next flimsy limb
                it jumps

No review of aerodynamic competence
or confidence by the Canada
goose in mid-flight
                it flies

Not one logistical checklist
for the acorn, seedling
or oak

                    it grows
each perfect as it is
just like
you

who
despite knowing
continues to plan

to check the list
ever preparing to
jump to fly to be

instead of jumping
flying
being.

THE OLD LESSON AGAIN (AND AGAIN)
- *after William Stafford*

And then one day
if you're lucky
or unlucky, or
you recognize a moment
of grace (or grace recognizes you)
you wake up to find
what you thought was
the way things are
is how you are, and
the real work begins
because how you are
doesn't reveal itself
in one fell swoop or
even two full sweeps
but rather one belief, view,
habit, lens, experience or
culture at a time, and just

when you think you
see clearly, that you
understand things as
they are, another veil falls,
an insight arrives, and you
realize you're capable of
yet another shift, other
transformations await,
further openings beckon,
subtle lenses still filter
your view and this is
the way it goes
the way things are
the way you are

the way it is

and recognizing this
you breathe deep,
relax a bit, are more
or less okay until
the next time you forget
the way things and you are
and perhaps awaken again,
remembering beliefs, views,
habits, lenses, experiences,
cultures, veils, insights, shifts
and transformations emerge
and fall away, emerge
and fall away, and that's
the way it is.

Afterwordledgments

In recent years, my work as a poet, writer, educator and coach has moved steadily in the direction of healing – at first quite 'accidentally' and then more intentionally. That these poems come together as part of my own 'healing narrative' at once surprises me and makes perfect, inevitable, sense.

I believe that I am, and we all are, always healing – whether towards the resolution of some specific experience or condition in our lives, or 'just' our habitual, perceived sense of separation from each other and the universe. Origin stories, whether religious, scientific or 'something else' in nature, tend to agree on *one beginning*. If you're reading this and you began separately, please share the details with the rest of us.

I am blessed with friends, colleagues and family who live remarkable stories – as loved ones suffer and die, health changes, chronology marches on, dreams fade, cherished beliefs lose their usefulness, and illusions give way to direct experience. We all live these stories, differentiated by timing, context and intensity for sure, and inevitably integrated by life, love and loss.

Each story speaks to and of our common humanity – that no one of us is in this alone, even when it feels as though we are. My initial intention was to name some of these 'ridiculously resilient' folks, but I thought there are just too many, and I'd inevitably leave someone out. And *then* I thought, yeah, well so what – what about the people I *do* include?

In the ridiculously resilient category, deep bows of admiration, love and respect go out to my cousins Christine, Paul, Rita and Tom Luna, Rob Francess, Tracey Burke, Joanna Burgess-Stocks, Kevin Houston, Vanessa Goettinger Vergnetti, Julie Flaherty, Jill Lang Ward, John Stoddart, Karin Hempel, Leslie Williams, Eileen Dulen-Jennings and David Rogers. Each of you, in your uniquely resilient way, inspires me.

I'm deeply grateful to Kent Frazier, Cam Gregg and Steve Benson, and blessed to have as friends, Morgan Smith, Larry Pisani, Janet Aalfs, Brec Morgan, Kim Salander, Bruce Tepikian, Jane Baniewicz, Chris Royer, Robert Gambardella, Fred Krawchuk, Tom Rubens, Lisa McCall, Autumn van Ord, Barbara Bitondo, Mike Beck, Rusty Gasparian, Christiane Meunier, Almudena Gonzalez, Bridgit Dengel Gaspard, Amy Phillips, Gayle Beyer, Alice McCarthy, Trebbe Johnson, Jim Arsenault, Michael Brant DeMaria, Ray DiCapua, Joe Woolley, Patti Reiser, Terry Walman, Alex Douds, Lois and Jim MacNaughton, Joel Kreisberg, Joan Ferraro – for "the story," all my Eufemia cousins (especially Steve, for Moving Day), and my favorites – *everyone I left out.*

The "Friends for ( ) Years Club Members," Tom Rogers (38), Jerry Houston (45), Mike Philp (47), and Paul Tepikian (55) just won't quit, lucky for me.

Finally, the three wild cards: Lucile Tepikian, 94 years young as I type this; Aunt Ann Luna, 95 years and counting; and Antoinette – Aunt "Babe" – Cardamone, Godmother, phone pal and confidante, who's been at it since January 5, 1917, approaching the beginning of her 100th year as this book goes to print.

I love you all.

I believe Icarus was not failing as he fell,
but just coming to the end of his triumph.

- Jack Gilbert, "Failing and Flying"

About the Author

Reggie Marra is a native of Yonkers, New York. This is his third volume of poetry and his seventh title overall. As this book goes to press, he serves as Creative Director and is on the core faculty at the Teleosis Institute, he is a Mentor Coach with the International Coach Federation, Integral Coaching Canada, and the M.A. in Health and Wellness Coaching program at Maryland University of Integrative Health, and has served on the visiting faculty at The Graduate Institute in the M.A. in Consciousness Studies program.

Since 1996 he has presented his work for the National Association for Poetry Therapy, the National Speakers Association, the Iona College Spirituality Institute and the Transformative Language Arts Network, among others. Reggie has taught hundreds of poetry-writing classes in schools throughout the northeastern U.S., including his work with the Connecticut HOT Schools program, and he has been a trainer with and a judge for the National Endowment for the Arts Poetry Out Loud competition for high school students.

Way back in the 20th Century he worked for 21 years as a high school teacher and basketball coach and as a college administrator.

He enjoys finding ways to alleviate unnecessary suffering for the willing, including himself, through writing, teaching, coaching, healing and humor – and any other means necessary.

You can learn more at http://reggiemarra.com, where you can also find his email address if you'd like to offer a testimonial for these poems.

Reggie welcomes your review of this book on Amazon as well.

CHRISTMAS, A TIME OF SORROW

There is a time of the year,

When multi-colored lights are lighted,

Trees are removed from the soil, and taken home
    to be decorated.

Toys and other gifts are placed in boxes beneath the tree,

And white flakes of snow drop from the skies,

Moving us into a new world.

Some of us wish to go on into this world.

Others would rather remain in the old world,
    being afraid of what the new might bring.

And all the people are warm and friendly,

Coming together to honor the Birth of the Son of God.

That's the real reason for the warmth and friendliness,
    isn't it?

The gifts and lights are simply outward, insignificant signs
    of our happiness at His Birth, aren't they?

There is another time,

When rows of candles are lighted and the soil itself
    is dug up.

And a wooden box is placed beneath the soil, and in the box
    he dreads the loss of heaven and the pains of hell.

Many tears drop from many eyes as he is sent on his way
    to a new and different world.

And now, as the one in the box stands before Him to be judged,
    he seems sorrowful and humbled.

He is sorry for his sins because they offend Him, whom he loves.

That's the real reason for his sorrow, isn't it?

Dreading the loss of heaven and the pains of hell are only
    small hints to guide us, aren't they?

So all you neon people at Christmas, and all you suddenly
    sorrowful souls on your death beds,

Join hands.

Reg Marra
12/1/70

www.ingramcontent.com/pod-product-compliance
Lightning Source LLC
Chambersburg PA
CBHW021200100426
42735CB00046B/758